Nag Nag Nag

Megan and Emmett Volume I

By Kathy Steinemann

Print Edition
ISBN 978-1-927830-14-7

Cover by Kathy Steinemann

Foreword
R. L. Black

Dedicated

To all the married couples
who bicker and snipe
but forgive the
cookie crumbs in bed.

Thank-You

Many thanks to R. L. Black for writing the foreword. It was a pleasure to work with you.

I would also like to thank all the married couples out there who provided fodder for this book, and the many Scribophile writers who critiqued my work. I couldn't have done it without your advice and assistance.

Table of Contents

Foreword

It has been said that "humor heals", and that "a merry heart does good like a medicine". If this is true, and I suspect it is, then doctors all over the world should be prescribing this book!

The first time I had the pleasure of reading a Megan and Emmett story—I believe it was "Nag, Nag, Nag", the first story in this collection—I was hooked and had to have more. Thank goodness the author had more up her sleeve!

Emmett and Megan are like your favorite sitcom couple. (Hint, hint, Hollywood: this would make a great television show!) Think Archie and Edith Bunker meet Al and Peggy Bundy. They gripe, they argue, and what Emmett does with that butter—well, I won't tell you about that! But in the end we know they love each other. And the laughter and love keep us running back for more—that, and the butter.

The pieces in this collection are all quick reads; you can read one while you're having your morning coffee, or waiting for an appointment, or standing in line. Or you can curl up in your favorite spot and read the whole thing! Some of the stories, like "Nag, Nag, Nag", will have you roaring with laughter. And others, like "Valentine Verdict", will make you believe in the power of love.

It has been a privilege to work with the author as a critique partner, and to write this foreword, but the greatest privilege has been as a reader. Many thanks to the author for bringing this unforgettable couple to life. Long live Megan and Emmett!

R.L. Black
EIC, *Unbroken Journal*, & *Unlost Journal*

R. L. Black lives in Tennessee with her handsome husband and sweet little boy. She is EIC of *Unbroken Journal* and *Unlost Journal*, and her own writing has been published in journals across the Web and in print. You can find her at rlblackauthor.tumblr.com, where she blogs and reblogs about writing, *LOST*, and art.

Introduction

If you're allergic to laughter, get your meds ready. *Nag Nag Nag* will exercise your laugh muscles. It might even make you wet your pants.

Megan and Emmett share many of the same quirks and problems as other married couples. The way they deal with them might take you aback.

Discover how Emmett copes with Megan's nagging. Learn how Megan treats telemarketers. Her once-in-a-lifetime offer makes them hang up. Every time. Will Emmett ever fix the blasted dishwasher? You'll be shocked when you realize why it broke in the first place. And how does he get around Megan's cat rules?

Granddaughters, Violet and Lisa, provide a few surprises and chuckles too, with the unique perspectives of youth. Their widowed mother, Marsha, is determined to raise her daughters right. That means healthy food like broccoli. Yuck! The difference between broccoli and snot is that kids don't eat broccoli.

And we can't forget Sabrina, the Siamese cat. You'll find her meowing and purring her way into your heart as she careens around corners and wins the affections of the most unlikely characters.

Nag Nag Nag will entertain you with laughs, tears, and unexpected twists.

Nag, Nag, Nag

This is a reprint of Kathy's story that was published in Fine Linen Magazine on April 15, 2015.

Emmett flipped to the sports section of the newspaper.

Megan's strident voice stung his ears. "For crying out loud. You got toast crumbs all over the place again." She scraped at the butter with a knife to remove the errant flecks of brown. "Smarten up."

He ignored her.

"Did you hear me?"

"The whole blasted neighborhood heard you." He lowered his paper to the table. The front page landed on top of the butter dish.

Her chin hardened into an orange-peel pattern. "You did that on purpose!"

"Did what?"

"Mucked up the butter again."

He rolled his eyes. "It was an accident."

Megan muttered as she took the dish to the sink and spooned the yellow mess into the trash. "That's it. I'm getting you your own butter dish. Then you can dirty it up as much as you want."

Emmett mumbled, "Nag, nag, nag."

She turned and propped her hands on her hips. "*What* did you say?"

He shrugged. "I said I won't wipe my toast knife on the dish anymore, and I'll keep the newspaper away. You happy?"

"I'll believe it when I see it."

Sabrina, their Siamese cat, jumped onto the table. Megan sideswiped her back onto the floor. "Bad kitty."

She slammed a cupboard. "I've gotta go shopping and buy toilet paper. You used it all up—*again*—without writing it on the grocery list. Oil the hinges on the front door while I'm gone. It's squeaking again. And put some fresh butter in the dish."

He nodded, and waited for the noisy squeal signaling her departure, before he retorted, "Nag, nag, nag. Never any peace around here."

After a vain attempt to concentrate on the crossword puzzle, Emmett pushed away from the table. "Suppose I'd better look at the door, or I'll never hear the end of it."

He rummaged through the freezer for a pound of butter and ran it over both door hinges while he moved the door back and forth a few times. The squeaking stopped. *Perfect.*

The glint from a button on his motorcycle jacket in the entryway caught his attention. He looked at the stick of butter in his hand. Back at the jacket. Somewhere he'd read that butter was good for lubricating leathers. "What the heck."

Ten minutes later, Emmett stood and admired his work.

He cocked his head. *This morning's health column said shea butter is good for athlete's foot. I wonder ...* He slipped off his socks. Wrinkled his nose as the rancid odor drifted up to his nostrils. Then he peeled back the foil wrapper and rubbed butter over his angry red toes. Soon both feet were coated in a greasy layer of yellow.

Sabrina sniffed at one of his toes. He jerked his foot away. "Hey, that tickles. Here." He held out his hand. The cat licked at the butter, with closed eyes and an audible purr. "Good kitty."

He pulled his smelly socks back over his feet. *They feel better already.*

He sneezed as he deposited what was left of the butter into the dish. Sneezed again. *Crap. I must be getting a cold.* He smoothed the butter with a knife, lowered his head, and checked the dish from several angles. *Good.* His studious expression brightened into a smile. *What she doesn't know won't hurt me.*

He found his cell phone hiding under the paper and texted Megan: *Switching to margarine. Pick some up. You can have the butter.*

Emmett grabbed the newspaper and flipped to the cartoon section.

Counting the Minutes

Emmett can't wait to retire. Only 8655 minutes left to go.

Emmett glared at his watch. Fifteen minutes until quitting time. Fifteen minutes plus six workdays until retirement. *Saturday, Sunday, Monday, Tuesday, Wednesday, Thursday ... I wonder how many minutes that is.*

He punched the numbers into his phone calculator, and his eyes widened. *Including the rest of this shift: 8655.* He repositioned himself in the grader seat and grimaced. Pain shot down his leg.

Bouncing around in heavy equipment for three decades had jostled his bones so much he felt like a massive bruise every day when he went home from work. His back ached. His right elbow throbbed. His neck hurt from craning it over his shoulder to watch for obstacles and idiot drivers.

Emmett sighed.

He couldn't wait to hang up his safety vest and hard hat: Fishing trips with the guys. Hot afternoons under the willow tree in the back yard, with a cold brew in hand and the cat on his lap. Sleeping in every morning.

Fourteen minutes left.

I'd better get my butt back to the public works yard.

The opening bars from "Witchy Woman" blasted from his cell phone.

"Hi, sweetie. What do you want me to pick up from the store *this* time?"

"Some new vacuum bags. Then when you get home I need help moving furniture so I can get rid of all the cat hair. We need lawn garbage bags too, so you can clean the gutters and gather the leaves after you rake the yard tomorrow."

"Aw, c'mon."

"... and washers for the hose. The driveway needs to be power-washed and ... "

"Whoa! I need to find a pen and a piece of paper to write down all this crap. And I have to work this weekend. I told you that a month ago."

"I'm sure John can give you the weekend off. They owe you after all the extra shifts you've worked for the last thirty years."

~*~

Five minutes left.

Emmett nosed his grader into the equipment bay and shambled through the public works building to his boss's office. "John, Megan has a whole crap-load of work she needs help with this weekend."

"Don't even think about asking for time off. We're short-handed. Brock is sick and Werner is on holidays."

Emmett grinned. "Thanks, boss. I knew I could depend on you one last time."

Birthday Cake Blahs

This is an experimental form of flash fiction, a literary snack, if you will. Some might even call it kitchen fiction. Emmett decides to try a recipe he found on the Internet. What could go wrong?

If I hurry, I can bake Megan a birthday cake before she gets back from her mother's place. Blasted bakery wants way too much money. Who do they think I am? Donald Trump? Nah. Too much hair to pass for The Donald. Heh heh. Maybe I should make a toupee from my barber clippings and sell it to him.

Ingredients:

1/2 cup brown sugar

Only half a cup? I'll double it. Megan never makes it sweet enough.

1/2 cup all-purpose flour

We're just about out of flour. And duct tape for the toilet seat. And we need more beer for my fishing trip. No time like the present. I'll pick up some cat food for Sabrina, too.

Where did I leave the car keys? Not on the hook. Not in my coat pocket … Ah! There they are—in Sabrina's bed. Maybe I should pick up a couple of catnip mice as well.

~*~

Crap! Sabrina spread brown sugar and flour everywhere. But she sure looks happy lickin' all the sugar off her fur. Gotta clean up the mess before I can even think about baking …

Now, where was I?

1/2 cup brown sugar
1/2 cup all-purpose flour
1/4 cup peanut butter

What kinda BS cake is this?

Just my luck. Peanut Butter Delight. Shoulda paid more attention when I downloaded the recipe. Damn allergies! Don't need the trots and hives. Last time I ate peanuts, took me days to stop itching. The guys told me my lips were so big I could kiss my own butt.

Don't have enough time to find another freakin' recipe or run back to the store. I need to find something soft and creamy. Molasses?

When I mix it with flour, it's sort of the same consistency.

Yeah. That'll do.

3 Tbsp. margarine or butter

Humph. No butter left. Used it all up when I greased the garage door rollers. Margarine it is.

2 cups all-purpose flour

More flour? Oh, the flour before was for the topping. This is for the batter. Stupid recipe.

1 cup brown sugar

Thanks to the cat, no brown sugar left. I should have known better than to leave anything on the counter. I'll mix white sugar with cinnamon.

Yeah. That looks okay.

2 tsp. baking powder
1/2 tsp. baking soda
1/4 tsp. salt
1 cup milk

Can't use milk. Wouldn't want to be passing gas on Megan's birthday. After supper, she'll expect to celebrate in the bedroom. Heh heh heh. Guess that's one of the reasons I married her.

Wonder how the cake would taste with beer instead of milk. Maybe I'll get famous for inventing a new dessert.

Hey! Is it supposed to foam like that?

1/2 cup peanut butter

What's with all the peanut butter in this blasted recipe? I'm already using molasses for the topping. Marmalade maybe?

Yeah, marmalade mixed with flour. Seems all right. Even kinda looks like peanut butter.

2 eggs

The doctor told me I have to watch my cholesterol. But just this once … What the heck. If I'm gonna do it, might as well go all in. I'll use four eggs.

1/4 cup margarine or butter

This margarine does NOT taste "just like butter". Someone should force-feed it to a few advertisers and make 'em come up with a better slogan.

Directions for Topping:

In a bowl stir together 1/2 cup brown sugar and 1/2 cup all-purpose flour. With a pastry blender or 2 knives, cut in 1/4 cup peanut butter and 3 Tbsp. margarine or butter until crumbly.

Hmm. Guess it tastes okay. Not crumbly like Megan makes it. Does gloppy count? I wonder what she uses instead of peanut butter. Her cakes are always delish, even if they aren't sweet enough.

Directions for Batter:

In a separate bowl, stir together 2 cups flour, 1 cup brown sugar, baking powder, baking soda, and salt. Add milk, 1/2 cup peanut butter, eggs, and 1/4 cup margarine or butter. Beat with mixer on low speed until blended. Beat at high speed for another 3 minutes, scraping sides of bowl often.

Doesn't look or smell anything like it should. I'll add some cocoa. And a smidgen of coffee. Decaf.

Blech! Maybe it'll taste better after it's baked.

Pour batter into greased 13"x9"x2" baking pan. Spread evenly. Sprinkle with topping mixture. Bake at 375° about 30 minutes or until a toothpick inserted near the center comes out clean.

Let's see. My feet are eleven inches long. If I can find a cake pan big enough to put my foot into, with a couple inches to spare …

Yeah. This one should work.

Running out of time. I'll turn the oven up to 500° and pick some flowers while I'm waiting.

~*~

Gah! Damn smoke. This cake is crap. The old broad's more talented than I gave her credit for.

If I hurry, I can buy her a birthday cake before the bakery closes. Better order a dozen roses, too.

Auld Lang Syne

Megan's surprise for Emmett turns out to be more of a surprise than she expected.

Emmett dropped his keys after unlocking the front door. While he was fumbling to return them to his pocket, Megan switched on the lights. Several people shouted, "Surprise!"

He turned toward her and grumbled in an almost inaudible voice, "You know how much I hate surprise parties."

Plastering a fake smile on his face, he shook hands and listened to a barrage of "happy retirement" congratulations.

His grumbling continued during dinner. "Vegetables. Blech! Are you trying to kill me for the insurance? And what's this organic dreck?"

After supper, everyone sang "Auld Lang Syne". He responded with a grimace.

A frown swept over his face after Megan lit the sparkler on his retirement cake. An errant spark set the curtains ablaze, and the room erupted into a frantic burst of chaos.

Derek dropped his drink in his lap and swatted a fleck of ash from his hair. Aldona stumbled over Derek's feet as she ran from the fire. She tripped face-first into a piece of cake that had flown onto the floor.

Larry wrestled the water-cooler bottle off its stand and splashed everything between him and the curtains. John grabbed the fire extinguisher.

Sabrina, Megan and Emmett's Siamese cat, clawed up the sofa, yowling her displeasure at the sudden wetness.

Kathy careened into Lorraine. Lorraine fell against Keith, knocking off his glasses. Bruno grabbed Kat's cane and started yanking down curtains. A flying ember landed in Al's mustache. He slapped at it and gave himself a nosebleed.

Within moments, the flames and festivities had been snuffed out like a trampled cigar butt. John put down the extinguisher to rub at the soot on his chin.

Smoke and steam hung in the air. The sickening smell of burnt mustache tickled Emmett's throat. He coughed.

Then he looked at the dour expressions and chuckled. His chuckle escalated into raucous laughter. He doubled over, face red, tears streaming down his face. "Megan, this is absolutely the best party I've ever had."

Once-in-a-Lifetime Offer

Experimental, dialogue-only format.
Have you ever tried Megan's technique for discouraging
telemarketers?

"Good evening, ma'am. Is this Megan Walpole?"

"Yes ...?"

"How are you today?"

"Well, now that you ask, I stubbed my big toe on the bottom step this morning, and I'm having a flare-up of my arthritis. My back isn't so great, either. Nice of you to ask."

"The reason I called is because your name was drawn from a random pool, and you're the winner of an all-expense paid trip to Hawaii."

"Well you can just tie a rock to my name and throw it right back into that random pool where you found it. Why do you guys always call while I'm in the middle of making supper?"

"May I call you Megan?"

"Young man, you can call me Al; you can call me gorgeous; you can even call me late for supper. Just don't call me back."

~*~

"Good evening again, ma'am. Um ... Oh yeah ... Here we go ... Ahem. This is a once-in-a-lifetime offer. Let me explain what I can do for you."

"First time, isn't it? Do you think you have a kinky old lady here? Well, the kinky part is right. Let me explain what *I* can do for *you*. Never mind. Five minutes with me and you'd have a heart attack."

"Uh ..."

"Ta-ta."

~*~

"Ma'am, I, uh ... I want to tell you about a special promotion Caliber Roofing and Siding has in your area. When you hire us to install our premium-quality aluminum siding on your home and allow us to display our sign on your lawn, you'll receive 10 percent off our professional installation AND that free trip to Hawaii. It'll just take a few minutes of your time."

"Whoa! Catch your breath and take as long as you want, sweetie. Give me *all* the details. I *like* it slow. Supper's in the oven now, and I have lots of time."

~*~

"Hey, Emmett. Come here a minute. I just put this telemarketer on mute while he goes through his spiel."

"You going to talk sexy and ask him what he's wearing like you did with the last poor schmuck?"

"Nope. I've got something even better in mind. Listen and learn. Ready?"

"... and then we—"

"Hold on. Before you go any further, I should tell you I live in a brick house. You'd have a tough time installing aluminum siding on that."

"Uh ..."

"But you just go right on talking. You've got a nice voice, and I haven't had anyone to chat with for over six days."

"Six days? Oh I'm—"

"Yup. Ever since I chopped up my husband with an ax. He kept on yabbering when I was trying to make supper. His body is in the garage freezer along with all his stinky fish bait. Do you think your guys could dispose of his corpse for me? Then they could install siding on the garage. It's not made of brick. I'll pay good. Once-in-a-lifetime offer. My husband had a generous life insurance policy."

"Uh ..."

"Young man? Young man? ... Guess he hung up."

"Heh heh. Flattened by the Megan train. Almost feel sorry for the kid. How about comin' down the hall and showin' *me* some of that kinky stuff?"

Shopping Tutorial

Emmett tries to teach Megan the right way to shop.

Megan grumbled, "Stupid old hypochondriac."

Emmett snatched the peanut butter away from her. "That's chunky. Buy the smooth stuff. You know I'm allergic to peanuts."

She shook her head as she plucked another jar from the supermarket shelf. "How long before you go on your fishing trip?"

With a knowing smirk, he checked his cell phone. "I just downloaded an app for that. Six days, twenty hours, fifteen minutes, twenty-two seconds."

Megan gritted her teeth. *Not soon enough!*

Emmett puffed out his chest. "I'll teach you how to do the shopping efficiently. Listen and learn, honey."

"*You* listen. I've been doing this on my own for forty years. You've been retired for four days, and suddenly you know everything about shopping?"

He cocked his head. "I've been researching it on the Internet. You've been doing it all wrong."

Megan sighed.

Emmett's eyes brightened. "Oh, look." He stopped, then frowned as he scrutinized brand after brand of soda. "Maybe we should pick up juice instead. I had to switch to decarbonated coffee, and these all say 'carbonated' on the label." He shuffled to the next section and grabbed several boxes of orange juice.

Megan suppressed a giggle while she checked the shopping list. "We need cat food."

"Right." He navigated to the pet-food aisle.

She reached down for their usual brand, but Emmett swiped her hand away. "That stuff's junk. Our little Sabrina deserves the best. Here. We'll get this."

"The most expensive stuff on the shelf? You care more about Sabrina than you care about me!"

"If you want quality, you gotta pay for it." He dumped a dozen cans into the cart.

Megan put them back on the shelf and replaced them with Sabrina's usual fare. "But I'm the one who has to worry about the grocery budget."

"Whatever."

They meandered into the snacks section.

Megan grappled for the cart. "You don't need anything from this aisle. Look at your waistline."

Emmett scowled at her and took the cart back. "I want cookies."

She chucked a bag of cheap cookies on top of the cat food. "Maybe you should go and live with the Cookie Monster."

He glared at her. "Not those. You know I hate them. The chocolate ones with the white filling." He replaced Megan's choice with three bags of his favorites. "And these chocolate bars."

Megan squinted at him. "We're out of toothpaste."

"We got lots left. The tube's almost full."

"I … need it to clean my jewelry."

Emmett shrugged. "Guess it's cheaper than jewelry cleaner." He waited, fingers tapping on the handle, while she picked out a giant tube. Then he pushed the cart into the dairy section. "See, you gotta be organized. Cold stuff last. I'll teach you yet."

So says the guy who can't find his glasses when they're sitting on his nose. "Really, Mr. Big-Shot Know-It-All?"

Emmett scanned the shelves. "Where's the latex-free milk? I think cow milk's been causing my gas."

"Well, by all means, let's find it. Quick! This is what you need." Megan handed him a carton of lactose-free milk. He took it and added three more cartons to the cart.

Emmett smiled as his gaze traveled farther down the aisle. "Oh, look! Heavy cream. I want to use that in my coffee from now on. The artificial crap gives me heartburn."

"But heavy cream contains lact— Never mind." She stifled a titter.

Emmett placed the cream in the bottom of the cart and headed toward the express lane.

Megan grabbed his arm. "We've got more than ten items. We can't go in there."

"Sure we can. Watch and learn." He nodded at the cashier. "Good morning, miss."

"Good morning, sir. Did you find everything you need?"

"Everything 'cept a new wife. You applying for the job?"

The girl blushed and stared at Megan with a *help me* plea in her eyes.

Megan cleared her throat. "Emmett, cut it out or I'll give you a good reason to find a new wife."

He hung his head.

The girl glanced at the cart. "I'm sorry, sir, but you have more than ten items. You'll have to go to the next checkout."

"Waddaya mean?" He gestured at the cart. "Peanut butter, juice, cat food, cookies, chocolate bars, toothpaste, milk, and cream. I reckon that makes eight items. Below our limit."

The frazzled-looking girl glanced around as though she might call a supervisor. But after a short pause, she rang the items through, shaking her head as she worked.

Emmett nodded at Megan. "You putting this on your credit card? It has air miles."

Not enough to take me where I want to go. Megan approached the terminal while Emmett loaded the groceries into their recycle bags.

The trace of a smile played at the corner of the cashier's lips. "Have a good day, ma'am."

Megan harrumphed. "Not when I'm shopping with him."

~*~

Emmett lowered the grocery bags to the kitchen floor, and Megan started unpacking, placing the cat food on the counter. It was sopping wet.

She pulled the rest of the groceries out of the bag. Sabrina lapped at the white drips that escaped to the floor. "Emmett, why did you put the heavy cream on the bottom of the bag? The carton burst. You'll have to buy some more."

"The Internet says the heavy stuff should always go on the bottom."

She sighed. "Excuse me. I need to go clean up a mess."

"It's not that bad. It'll only take you a couple of minutes."

"Not the cream. The mess I'll make when I beat my head against the wall."

He threw on his coat. "You don't have to be so melodramatic. I'll go get some more." The door slammed behind him.

Megan grabbed the bag of cookies, scraped the cream filling from each one, and replaced it with toothpaste. Then she unwrapped one of the chocolate bars and substituted it with ex-lax.

She smiled. *Maybe next time I go grocery shopping he'll stay home.*

Dishwasher Dispute

What's the matter with the bleepin' dishwasher?

Emmett banged his glass on the counter and wiped the milk mustache from his upper lip. "What's for supper?"

Megan glared at him. "A good husband would put his glass in the dishwasher."

"Never claimed to be a good husband." He ducked when she threw the dishrag at him.

Her nostrils flared. "I have to do everything around here, you lazy bum."

"But you do such a good job of everything. The vacuuming. The cooking. Washing the dishes." He ducked again to dodge the dishtowel.

Megan's glare grew into a scowl. "The least you could do is scrape your plate before putting it on the counter."

"Nag, nag, nag."

She sighed. "The dishwasher's on the fritz. Again. Every time I go to visit Mom for a couple of days, I come back to a dishwasher that doesn't drain properly and two sinks full of dirty dishes."

"You're on the fritz? Take two aspirin. Always works for me."

"Smart ass! I'm not your maid. And I'm serious about the damn dishwasher. It's not working right, and it smells funky."

Emmett's smile turned smug as he put his plate on the floor in front of their Siamese cat. "Here, Sabrina, you lick this clean so Mommy'll get off Daddy's case about scraping it."

"Emmett!"

He bit his lip. "Maybe I can fix it. I'll take a look—after I finish reading my paper."

"Or you could buy a new one."

"Nah. It's not that old."

Her face reddened. "Not that old? It's older than that expensive suit you bought for Dad's funeral. And he died sixteen years ago."

"Expensive? I'm not the one who spends money like it grows on trees. What about that nice dress I paid for when your mother got married again?"

"I got that on sale! The most expensive thing you ever bought me was this stupid dishwasher. What a nice, romantic gift, cheapskate."

He smirked. "You're welcome."

Megan stormed out of the kitchen.

Emmett shuffled to the dishwasher. "Guess I should take a look. Darned thing worked fine yesterday when I washed my undershorts and socks in it."

Cat Burglar

*What is Sabrina up to? She seems determined to keep Megan
awake.*

Scratch.

"Meow."

Scratch-scratch-scratch.

Megan pulled the duvet up to her chin and mumbled, "Go
away, Sabrina. You're not getting any more food."

There was a thump against the bedroom door.

Silence.

Megan sighed. *I wonder how much longer she needs to stay on
this stupid diet.* She snuggled closer to Emmett and dreamed of
emaciated felines trying to open cans of tuna with their claws.

Thud.

Skitter.

"Meow."

Darned cat. Is she going to keep this up all night? Megan
listened for a few moments before sinking into another dream, this
time of Sabrina on a treadmill, trying to catch a fish dangling from
a string.

Rattle.

Gallop-gallop-gallop.

Thump.

*Freakin' Sabrina. Should I give in? No way. I can't stand her
stinky cat farts. Maybe I should ...* The drone of Megan's snoring
filled the room.

"Meow."

Rustle.

Thud.

Rattle-rattle-rattle.

Megan threw a pillow at the door. *For crying out loud! That brat's going to be in deep doo-doo when I get my hands on her.*

She waited for several minutes, determined not to get out of bed. Except for the sound of a vehicle somewhere in the street, the night was noiseless.

Megan drifted back into a fitful sleep.

~*~

The cool of early morning chilled Megan's nose. Her tongue tasted like stinky socks. *Guess Sabrina finally gave up.* She glanced at the alarm clock. Blinked. *Damn.* She shook Emmett's shoulder.

He shrugged her hand away. "Mmph. What did you do that for?"

"You'll be late for work."

"I'm retired now. Remember?"

Megan groaned. "Oh. Yeah. Sorry. Didn't sleep much. Sabrina kept me up half the night."

"Where is the little brat?" Emmett kicked off the covers. "Might as well make some coffee and sit with her for a while. I'll never be able to get any shuteye now."

"It takes an explosion to wake *you* up, but please be quiet. *I've* gotta get some sleep."

"I'll try. 'Cept you can hear a mouse sneeze from three blocks away."

Megan was already asleep.

Emmett threw on his robe and wiggled his toes into his slippers. As he shuffled to the dark kitchen, he almost tripped over a catnip mouse and an empty treat ball that Sabrina had dragged into the hallway.

An icy breeze nibbled at his knees. He reached toward the cupboard for the coffee, and glanced at the window. It was open. *Crap. Megan must have forgot to shut it last night.* He pushed it closed and headed for the light-switch. A loaf of bread lay on the counter, plastic wrap chewed through. *Megan's plan isn't working very well. The cat needs to come back into the bedroom with us, farts or no farts.*

Something soft squished under one foot. Emmett grimaced and pulled off his sock. He sniffed. *Tuna. Did Megan— Nah. She's the one who insisted Sabrina go on a diet. How in blazes did this get here?*

Unease crept up his spine and tingled to his ears. He scanned the kitchen. Two empty tuna cans were wedged into the corner between the stove and dishwasher.

A half-exhaled breath stalled in Emmett's throat. Even in the dim light, he could see that the mason jar full of twenties was missing from the china cabinet.

He pulled a sharp knife from the cutlery drawer and edged toward the telephone, hyperventilating as he dialed.

"911. What is your emergency?"

Emmett whispered, gaze darting to every corner and crevice. "Someone broke into our house, and they might still be here."

"One moment. ... Police have been notified and are on en route from four blocks away. Please remain on the line. Your name, sir?"

"Emmett. Emmett Walpole."

"Are you alone?"

"No. My wife's here too."

"Is there someplace you can get to with a lock on the door, Emmett? Like a bathroom?"

"The bedroom. It's just down the hall."

"Go to the bedroom, lock yourself in, and stay as far away from the door as possible. Do not try to find or engage the intruder."

"But what about Sabrina?"

"Have your wife wait in the bedroom with you."

"Sabrina's our cat."

"Don't worry about the cat, Emmett. It's imperative that you and your wife remain safe. Do you understand?"

He muttered, "Yes. I'm on my way."

He unlocked the back door, flattened himself against the wall, and listened for any sign of movement, hoping for Sabrina to come barreling around the corner.

His heart pounded like an unbalanced washer load against his ribs as he crept down the hall. *Damn. I can read the headlines already: "Homeowner Dies from Coronary Before Police Arrive."* He tried to calm his breathing, but felt as though he were broadcasting his presence through a megaphone with every rasping pant.

He passed the living room. Stopped. Backed up. Peered inside.

A shadowy shape slumbered in the loveseat, mouth open, snuffling. The sound reminded Emmett of a piglet rooting in a feed trough. Sabrina was cuddled next to the man, rolled up like a cinnamon bun tight against his waist. A lumpy pillowcase lay on the floor, silverware chest and computer tablet peeking from its mouth, next to an empty bottle of rum.

Emmett scowled. *Well, I never.*

The click of the back door opening broke the silence, and Sabrina's ears twitched. She snuggled closer to the intruder, who was now wide awake, stunned eyes staring at Emmett. A flurry of voices, beginning with Megan's, blared from the darkness.

"Emmett, what's going on? Why are the cops here?"

"Sir, get out of the way."

"We have this under control."

"Get down on the ground. Now!"

The man in the loveseat struggled to a seated position and raised his hands high over his head. Sabrina eyed everyone within range and licked her paws.

The man trembled, then slurred, "Don't shoot. I'm unarmed, see? Don't hurt the cat."

One of the police officers flipped the light-switch. Sabrina blinked, bounded away from the burglar, and rubbed against Emmett's legs. Another officer dragged the man out of the loveseat and cuffed him.

Emmett picked up Sabrina. "No more skinny-minny kitty food for you, cat, no matter what Megan says. Nothing but gourmet from now on."

Megan's Cat Rules

Here's another piece of experimental flash fiction. Megan leaves a note for Emmett when she goes to visit her mother.

Don't let Sabrina up on the new loveseat. I covered it with plastic, but she might scratch through it.

Humph. Ten days trying to keep the cat off the loveseat just because it's new? The old loveseat used to be her favorite sleeping spot. How else is she supposed to break in furniture if she can't knead it? Does Megan think I'm a prison warden or something? I'll grab the cashmere blanket out of the cedar chest and throw it over the loveseat. Meg will never know.

Please, no cigars while I'm visiting Mom! The smoke isn't good for you or Sabrina. All it takes is one stogie to make the whole house reek. And don't think I won't find out. I WILL discover your stash one of these days.

Guess I'll have to smoke them outside. Her ignorance is my bliss, and she'll never find out where I hide 'em.

Keep the door to the sewing room closed. I don't want to find fabric swatches and spools of thread strewn all over the floor.

No problem. Why would I need to go into the sewing room? Except to grab a cigar. Ha ha. Hidden right under her nose at the bottom of the cedar chest.

No dairy for you or the cat. I emptied all the milk from the fridge so you won't be tempted. I'll buy more on my way home. You'll find a couple of cartons of almond milk next to the orange juice on the top shelf.

Can't blame her for being mad. After I gave Sabrina milk last week, she got diarrhea all over Meg's new outfit. Maybe I should buy Megan a gift certificate at the dress shop.

Charge your cell phone in the den. With the door closed so Sabrina doesn't chew on the wires.

It was my fault she chewed on the charger cord last time. Shouldn't have wiggled it in front of her nose. Better for Sabrina to take the rap than me, though. Megan can never stay mad at those pretty little kitty eyes. Maybe I can close the door and sneak a cigar or two in there. Meg never goes in except to clean.

Don't feed her catnip in the bathroom. Last time you did that, she drooled on the floor, unrolled the toilet paper all the way into the living room, and wrecked two of the guest towels.

But she was such a riot to watch, rolling all over the place, chasing her tail. And that drunken purr. Priceless! Guess my bathroom entertainment will have to be motorcycle catalogues. Hey, I haven't talked to Megan lately about buying a Harley. Maybe she'll be in a good mood when she gets back. Especially if I do everything on this darned list.

Don't let her drink from the toilet. Either keep the bathroom door closed, or the toilet lid down. Your choice. I just put a fresh chlorine tablet in the tank.

Crap. I thought with Megan gone, I'd be able to leave the lid up. Forgot about those bleachy things in the toilet tank. Why did I tell myself I'd be happy to go it alone for ten days?

Don't tease her. It makes her hungry. And your hands get all scratched up.

Roughhousing is good exercise. I don't mind a scratch or two. And getting her to run around in circles while she chases the red laser dot on her butt is good exercise, too.

And don't try to teach her swimming in the bathtub again. You KNOW cats hate water. If you want a pet to go fishing with you and the guys, we can get a dog.

Heh heh. A dog would probably bark at burglars instead of snuggling up to them. But Sabrina looked so funny when she jumped into the tub trying to catch that spider on the soap dish. Hmmmmmm. I might need to bathe her to wash the cigar-smoke smell out of her fur. If I get any scratches, I can say I was teasing her again. Better remember to dig the cat hair out of the drain, though.

Only put dried food down for her twice a day: 7 a.m. and 5 p.m. The premium diet food. No snacks in between. Give her ONLY one-quarter can of wet food at lunchtime.

I'll put it down from 7 a.m. to 4 p.m. and from 5 p.m. until bedtime. Oh, it's lunchtime now. Better get the wet food ready.

Blech! I don't know how Sabrina can stand this stuff. It smells awful. Tuna flavor. I wonder why they don't make mouse-flavored cat food. Maybe I should invent it. Wonder what mice taste like.

No snacks. None. Nada.

No snacks? She looks so sad when she paws at my leg with that plaintive meow. Breaks my heart. Does bacon count as a snack? Megan won't find out unless I tell her.

Kill any spiders you find so she doesn't get excited and climb the curtains. I just finished sewing up the rips she made in them last Thursday.

Oh, crap. Don't know how to get around this rule without squealing on myself. It wasn't a spider that set her off. I was shining the laser on the ceiling, and she chased it. Sabrina likes chasing spiders. If she's not allowed outside, the least I can do is let her hunt in the house. Besides, I hate squishing those creepy little eight-legged monsters.

Oh, I'm giving the cedar chest to Marsha. We loaded it into the trunk before I left, and I'm donating the contents to the thrift store. See you when I get back.

xoxoxoxoxo

Duck Tape

Granddaughter Lisa learns all about duct tape from Grampa Emmett.

Emmett nodded as he finished mending the dustpan. "Duct tape. It can fix anything."

His granddaughter Lisa plunked a slipper onto his lap. "This needs to be fixed too. It has a hole in the bottom. See? I want to help you put out the garbage. But the grass is all wet, and I don't wanna get my feet yucky."

Emmett grinned. "Afraid of a little water?"

"Grampa! Mommy told me I had to keep warm and dry so I don't get the flu. I don't wanna get wings and fly away."

He laughed. "No big deal. I'll just cover the hole with duct tape. We can buy you some new slippers later." He cut off a generous piece of tape and covered the hole. "There. Almost as good as new. And if you grow some wings, I'll tape 'em down."

Lisa beamed. She followed him, tiptoeing through the grass, as he rolled the trash bin down to the curb. "Grampa, you got big holes in your slippers. Aren't your feet wet?"

"Yup, just a bit."

"Can I fix them with duck tape too?"

"Duct tape, sweetie. It has a T sound at the end like plucked and clucked and chucked." He tickled her. "Duct. Duct. Duct."

She giggled. "*Duck* tape, Grampa. Duck tape keeps stuff dry like ducks' feathers when they go swimming."

They turned toward the house. Emmet's feet squished across the lawn, then across the kitchen, leaving a wet trail on the floor.

Lisa shook her head as she removed her slippers on the mat by the door. "Gramma's gonna get mad at you."

"Shhhhhh. We don't want to wake Gramma or your big sister. I'll clean it up in a sec. Gotta get out of these wet wool socks before they shrink on me." He peeled off the socks and threw them into a corner next to his gardening boots, which were still caked with dried mud from three days before.

She whispered, a scowl on her little face, "Gramma's gonna get *really* mad. She says laziness is worse than telling fibs."

"Gramma Megan is always nice when you come to visit. If she gets too loud, I can use the duct—"

"*Duck* tape. Duck. Duck. Duck."

Emmett chuckled. "I can use the duct tape to muzz—" He bit his lip. "Never mind. Did you know that some of the best inventions in the world happened because of laziness? Take the dishwasher, for instance. Some rich lady invented it because she didn't want to do the dishes, and her servants kept chipping her china."

"I like washing dishes and playing with the bubbles. But Mommy says I put too much soap in the water."

His smile broadened. "I bet you don't put soap in the microwave. Microwave ovens were dreamt up by some guy who was too lazy to make popcorn or eggs the old-fashioned way."

"Mommy 'sploded an egg once in the microwave. She used soap to clean up the mess."

"Good point. You have to be extra careful with eggs. In the old days, you couldn't put TV dinners in there either, because they had metal on them."

"What's the matter with metal?"

"Ooooooh, microwaves don't like metal stuff. I put a spoon in our microwave once. Got a real fireworks show right inside the kitchen. Nowadays, everything's made of plastic. Wasn't enough for people to have TV dinners you could cook in the regular oven."

"I like TV dinners, 'specially roast beef with gravy. Mommy makes them when she gets too busy."

"Another invention for lazybones. A lady cooked up TV dinners for people who didn't wanna do their own cooking." He grabbed the duct tape and scissors.

"Whatcha doin'?"

"Making you a raincoat. Your mommy forgot to pack one. The weatherman says it's gonna rain today."

Lisa's eyes grew wider as the roll emptied. She squinted with every crackling noise when a new piece of tape ripped off. Soon all that remained was an empty ring of cardboard. Emmett started on a new roll. Within minutes, he had a tot-sized raincoat on his lap.

She smiled. "It's neat."

"And it'll keep you dry. Like duck feathers."

"Can you make one for Sabrina too? Kitties don't like to get wet."

"Maybe later. Right now I have something more important to make." He cut, folded, twisted, and held out his hand.

"What is it?"

"A flower. How does it look?"

"It's pretty. Thank-you." Lisa stared at the faux daisy. "Grampa, sheep make wool, right?"

"Yup."

"And wool shrinks when it gets wet?"

"Sure does."

"So why don't sheep shrink when it rains?"

Emmett choked back a snicker. "*Duck* tape, sweetie. They make raincoats out of *duck* tape."

Nightmares

Megan and Emmett take their daughter and granddaughters
camping.

Marsha panted and lowered her backpack to the ground. The bear bells on one of the pack's straps jangled as it flopped over. "Escalators would have been nice on that last climb, Dad. You didn't tell us it would be such a long hike. The parking lot is right over there. Why couldn't we have parked closer?"

Emmett puffed, propped his hands on his knees, and grinned. "Good for the constitution. Hey, if an old man like me can do it, a forty-one-year-old spring chicken and her ten- and five-year-old chicks should be able to keep up with me and your mom. Look at her. She's hardly winded at all."

Megan wiped the sweat from her chin. "Says who?"

Marsha coughed. "And the girls and I carried most of your stuff."

Emmett replied, with a smirk, "Minor detail. Someone needed free hands to swat at mosquitos, and a clear head to watch out for piles of grizzly poop."

Lisa, the youngest granddaughter, toed a mound of rabbit turds. "Grampa, how can you tell if poop is grizzly poop?"

He tweaked her cheek. "They're the piles of poop with bells on top."

"Grampa, that's a fib ..." Her gaze wandered around the campsite as she rotated in a complete circle. "... isn't it?"

"Yup. But even if a grizzly sneaks up on us, I'll keep you safe. I have magic powers."

Ten-year-old Violet tsk-tsked. "Grandpa, magic is only in fairy tales. Right Grandma?"

Megan shrugged. "You never know. Where did fairy tales come from? Most stories have at least some truth in them. Maybe Grandpa's telling the truth." She elbowed Emmett. "This time."

He clutched his chest. "I'm hurt that nobody believes me. Oh, oh, oh. You're killing me with your doubt. Clap your hands to tell me you believe in me. Don't let me die. Clap. C'mon. Clap. Like you did for Tinkerbell."

The granddaughters giggled and began to clap.

"Not loud enough."

They clapped faster. Megan and Marsha joined in.

Emmett took his hands away from his chest. "That's better. It's nice to know that all my women believe in me." He grabbed a water bottle.

Lisa squirmed, and a pained expression came over her face. Violet hopped from one foot to the other. Abruptly, both granddaughters pulled at straps, opened packs, and rushed to get the tents erected.

Emmett's jaw dropped. He turned to Marsha. "You got 'em well-trained. What did you do? Promise them marshmallows?"

"Nope. Told them they couldn't go to the bathroom until the tents were set up."

The girls' quick movements looked like a high-speed video clip. Emmett rubbed the stubble on his chin.

Marsha beamed. "Look at them go. If they ran to the outhouse any faster, we'd have to replace their running shoes."

Megan laughed. "Well I never. Wish we'd thought of that when you were growing up. You always dawdled when we went camping."

Emmett harrumphed. "Putting up tents is nothing like it was in the old days. One minute and POOF, it's done. Let's see how long it takes to pack them up again."

"Sure, Dad." Marsha nudged his shoulder. "And you had to walk uphill both ways to school. Twelve miles there and twelve miles back. In fifty-below weather."

Megan's cheeks dimpled. She raised her eyebrows and motioned to Marsha. "Ready to set up for supper?"

"Yup. Wienie roast, here I come."

Violet and Lisa raced back along the path from the outhouse. Lisa tugged at Emmett's pant leg. "Can we play Frisbee now, Grampa?"

"Maybe after you pull on my finger."

"Grampa! You just wanna fart. But I wanna play Frisbee."

He sat on a log. "Nah. I'm bushed after that hike. Where do you rascals get all your energy? Do you want to hear a scary story before supper? Look. It's getting dark. The best time ever for stories."

Lisa squinted and shook her head.

Violet shoved her sister's shoulder. "Bwawk bwawk bwawk. It's only a story, you chicken."

Marsha urged Lisa forward with one hand. "Violet's right. You go and listen to a story while Grandma and I start a fire and get supper ready."

Emmett grinned. "Thanks, ladies. Need any belly button lint for fire starter?"

Megan gave him a dirty look.

He pointed a thumb in the direction of the girls' tent. "Good job on the tents, you two. Now how about getting into your PJs. And don't forget your housecoats. You need 'em to keep warm. And long sleeves so you have someplace to wipe your noses."

Violet giggled.

Emmett stared at the darkening sky. Not a cloud could be seen, and the moon glowed like a pearly Frisbee suspended in the latticework of branches above his head. Someone strummed an acoustic guitar in a nearby campsite. The gentle breeze carried an aromatic blend of wild roses, campfire smoke, and pine.

A smile played over his face as he remembered a day forty-some years ago when he and Megan had gone skinny dipping at midnight, the coldness of the water forgotten as they romped and splashed. They ended up making love in a soft bed of moss. And poison ivy. The relentless reminder of their torrid tryst was over a week of itching and squirming.

He chuckled.

Just when he was ready to check on the girls, they bounded out of their tent.

He patted the log in front of him, and both granddaughters sat down.

Emmett cleared his throat. "Once upon a time, in thick woods exactly like this, two white werewolves went on the prowl looking for supper. Their favorite meal was tender little children about your age."

Lisa slid closer to Violet.

"The wolves had huge fangs. Their fangs dripped saliva on the ground as they walked, leaving a silvery trail behind that glistened in the moonlight." His voice lowered. "One night, a night just like we're gonna have tonight, with a full moon and twinkling stars, the white wolves crept up on a campsite."

Violet nudged her little sister and spoke in a deep, somber tone, mimicking Emmett. "A campsite *just* like this one."

Emmett winked. "The wise creatures sat in the shadows, afraid to approach the fire, and listened to the grandfather telling a tale about two white werewolves. Then they looked at one another and wondered how he knew about them."

Violet and Lisa peered into the trees, their gaze darting in multiple directions.

He stirred the fire. "Their amber eyes followed every move of the grandfather. Should they skedaddle? No. The little girls looked *so* delicious and tender. And they smelled better than any children the hungry animals had ever seen before."

Lisa pouted. "I'm gonna use lotsa soap and get rid of my smell."

Emmett tousled her hair. "No need. The werewolves changed their mind. They were scared of the grandfather and his magical powers. They decided to leave and look elsewhere. As they slipped away, they stepped on a branch …" A spark popped. Both girls flinched. "… and made a cracking sound—just like that one."

Violet and Lisa bit their lips.

"Uh oh. Now everyone knew about the werewolves. They ran and ran and ran, their saliva trail growing fainter as they neared the lake. Then they dove into the water, transformed back into humans, and swam away as fast as they could, howling and splashing."

Violet frowned. "And what happened to the girls?"

"The little girls felt better, knowing their grandfather had great magic, and they slept well, dreaming about the wonderful things children always dream about when they're happy and safe."

Lisa beamed. "I like that story. It was magic. Just like you, Grampa."

Megan called from the picnic table. "Let's get started on salad and chips."

~*~

An owl hooted in the early dawn. Megan stretched. Ahhh. Fresh air and— What was that?

She pulled her robe tight and unzipped the tent.

Violet and Lisa huddled together on the logs in front of the fire.

Megan yawned. "What are you doing up so early?"

Violet hugged Lisa. "We had nightmares."

"Grandpa's silly story didn't scare you, did it?" Megan chuckled.

Lisa shook her head. "It wasn't a silly story, Gramma. We heard splashing and howling in the lake. We got up to look, and they were there. We saw them. Really. In the moonlight. We got scared and went to your tent so Grampa's magic could protect us, but you and Grampa must have been in the bathroom, so we slept with Mommy."

Megan snickered. "Yes, Grandpa certainly is magic."

She turned to Emmett, who was now standing behind her, and placed her arms around his neck. She whispered, "Guess we can't tell our grandkids we went skinny-dipping last night. Wouldn't want to give them even worse nightmares, would we?"

Broccoli Blues

Lisa is sick, and she's sure the broccoli caused it.

Marsha felt Lisa's forehead and took the thermometer from her mouth. "No temperature. Still have tummy cramps?"

Lisa grimaced. "Uh huh. I'm sorry I pooped my pants. I runned to the bathroom fast as I could, but my runs runned faster than me."

Marsha stroked her daughter's hair. "I don't think it's serious, but I'll see if I can make a doctor's appointment for you."

A giant rumbling noise exploded from under the covers. Lisa frowned. "It's okay. I just farted."

Her mother tsk-tsked. "What do you say?"

"Thank-you?"

"You excuse yourself when you fart."

"Oh. I forgot. 'Xcuse me. It's broccoli that made me sick. Grampa says the only difference between broccoli and snot is kids don't eat broccoli. And I hate it. It was yucky broccoli … broccoli … broccoli."

"Nice try. Broccoli is *healthy*, and I haven't served it for over a week. You had oatmeal for breakfast. That shouldn't make you sick. Next time I make broccoli, I'll smother it with a cheesy sauce."

Lisa threw off the covers and dashed for the bathroom.

Marsha followed her and waited by the open door. "Don't use so much toilet paper. You only have a tiny butt."

"Then you should use a *whole bunch* for *your* butt, Mommy."

Marsha sighed. Maybe it was time to stop finishing off the girls' leftovers. "You okay?"

"Yup. Now my tummy doesn't hurt."

Marsha grabbed the phone, had a lengthy discussion with the nurse, and scheduled a doctor's appointment for 3 p.m.

She considered cancelling after Lisa's dramatic improvement throughout the morning, but decided to be safe.

~*~

They arrived fifteen minutes early.

The waiting room overflowed with mothers and kids. A single father entertained his daughter. Occasionally his gaze wandered around the room. He reminded Marsha of a guy in the bar checking out the female customers. Not that she'd been to a bar recently. The man's eyes rested on her ring finger for a fleeting moment, spotted her wedding band, and flitted away.

Marsha slumped in her seat. It had been over five years since she'd lost Paul in a motorcycle accident while she was pregnant with Lisa, their second child. Some days she was so lonely. … But she wasn't ready to move on.

A little boy in the chair next to Lisa wiggled closer. "Are you sick?"

Lisa leaned away from him. "You're not s'pposed to get near people in the doctor's office. You might get Germans."

He giggled. "Germs, stoopid. 'Sides, I'm not sick. I got a itchy … you know." He rubbed at his crotch.

Lisa wrinkled her nose and stared at the boy's fingers. "Maybe you got germ-meezles on your weenie."

His mother cleared her throat and frowned at both kids. The boy bit his lip, continuing to scratch as he returned his attention to his handheld video game.

After a lengthy wait, the nurse summoned Marsha and Lisa to an examination room.

She closed the door and turned to Lisa. "I'm Faye. Your mommy told me all about your problems when I talked to her on the phone. She wants us to give you a complete checkup. Before Dr. Eunice gets here, I'll do a couple of things to make her job easier, okay?"

Lisa clung to Marsha's side for a moment before nodding.

Faye took Lisa's temperature and then patted the little girl's shoulder with gloved fingertips. "Can you stand on one foot?"

Lisa cocked her head. Lines formed on her brow. She stepped forward and stood on one of the nurse's feet.

Faye giggled. "That's not what I meant, sweetie. Can you stand like a ballet dancer, with one foot in the air and the other on the floor?"

Lisa pirouetted and stopped, arms outstretched, while she balanced on one foot.

"Good. Your balance seems fine. Now we'll check your hydration and sugar levels. I'm going to give you this plastic cup, and I'd like you to pee into it. The bathroom is down the hall to your right. Afterward, Mommy can bring you back here, and Dr. Eunice will be able to see you soon."

Lisa wrinkled her nose as she stared into the cup. "Do I hafta drink it?"

Faye snorted. "Nope. We put a little stick of cardboard in your pee and wait for it to turn color."

Lisa's eyes widened. "Is it magic cardboard?"

"Yup."

She smiled. "My Grampa is magic, but he doesn't have cardboard that changes color."

~*~

Bathroom duties complete, Marsha and Lisa waited for the doctor's knock. Dr. Eunice stepped into the room.

Lisa beamed. She could see a lump in the doctor's lab jacket. Candy. Dr. E. gave away the tastiest candies. Ever.

The doctor reviewed Lisa's chart. "So, diarrhea, gas, and tummy cramps, but no fever."

Lisa shook her head. "Direeeeeeeea!"

Mother and doctor shared an amused glance.

46

Dr. Eunice snickered as she typed a few characters on her laptop. "Has this happened before?"

Marsha shrugged. "A few times, but not this severe."

"Can you recall what Lisa ate each time she had these symptoms?"

"Oatmeal today … chocolate milkshake a couple of days ago … cornflakes over the weekend … ice cream cone last week. Something different each time."

Dr. Eunice's eyes crinkled. "Different, but not so different. All the foods you mentioned have something in common: dairy."

Marsha slapped her forehead. "Of course. I should have thought of that. Dad has lactose intolerance. Is there a test you can do to confirm it?"

Lisa squirmed. "I don't want any tests. Violet says they're horrrror-bull. You gotta study for them. And 'sides, I'm not in school yet."

The doctor grinned. "Not that kind of test. But no need to worry. We don't do lactose intolerance tests for kids. Just stay away from dairy or eat lactose-free products."

"I always stay away from Barry. He's mean."

Dr. Eunice handed Lisa a candy in a gleaming gold wrapper. "That's good. You stay away from Barry and milk and cheese and ice cream. I'll give your mommy a pamphlet that explains all about your tummy problem. Remember to take your vitamins and eat healthy."

"You mean I still hafta eat broccoli? And I can't have ice cream?" Her face wrinkled as though she had just sucked on a lemon.

"If you have a little bit of ice cream, it will give you gas, and you shouldn't get a tummy ache. But *only* a little bit. Okay?"

Lisa beamed. "Yeah. Then I can ask Grampa to pull on *my* finger from now on."

Broccoli with Acorns

Another broccoli encounter. Yucky stuff.

Lisa pushed her plate of broccoli-almond stir fry with Béchamel away and scrunched up her face. "Mommy, do I hafta eat this stuff? It still tastes yucky, even with the acorns and sauce."

Marsha tousled Lisa's hair. "Almonds, not acorns. I found the recipe on the Internet. Kids are supposed to love it. Your dad …" She bit her lip.

Violet wriggled her nose. "Well, I don't like it, either. I ate my meat and potatoes and some salad. May I please be excused from the table?"

Marsha nodded, took both plates, and contemplated for a few seconds. *Should I finish them off? No, I don't need the extra calories.* She scraped the remains into the garbage. "Let's go to the living room. I have something to show you."

Both girls scurried away as though they feared their mom might change her mind and serve up more of the awful concoction.

Marsha followed close behind. "No running in the house!"

They slowed to a walk.

Lisa pulled the photo of her father off the mantel. "Grampa says that's just like I'm gonna be when I grow bigger."

Marsha gazed at Lisa's freckles and matching freckle-brown hair. It wasn't the first time she had seen her husband in her daughter's face. She chuckled. "Yes, Grandpa's right. With your high forehead and that strong chin, you'll look like your daddy someday. The acorn doesn't fall far from the tree."

"Mommy, you said I grew in your tummy, not on a tree. Did you hafta swallow an acorn to grow me? Am I gonna turn into an acorn and get eaten by a squirrel?"

"No, uh—"

Violet tsked. "Mom means you look a lot like Dad." She took the photo, held it up to Lisa's face, and then buried her head in Marsha's blouse. "Why did it have to happen?"

"I don't know, sweetie. But you were so little. I thought by now you'd have forgotten …" She sniffled.

"I'll never forget. He used to sing me that song before he tucked me in at night. The one about the rubber dolly." She stepped back and swayed while she closed her eyes, arms cradling the photo as though she where rocking a baby

Lisa pursed her lips. "He sang it to me, too."

"No he didn't. You weren't born yet."

"Yes he did. I remember." Lisa stamped her foot.

Marsha squeezed between the girls. "Stop it! I had a cell-phone recording of Daddy singing the song. After he died, I used to play it for you every night. Until the phone got stolen a couple of years ago. Remember when I panicked because I thought I'd misplaced it, and then I called the police?" She wiped a tear from Lisa's cheek.

Lisa frowned. "I wish Daddy could sing it for me for real."

Violet put the photo back on the mantel. "Dad and Grandpa used to take turns giving me piggyback rides. When they got too tired, they fell on the floor and pretended they were dead. I tickled them until they laughed, then they tickled me back."

She stared at nothing, unfocussed. "I remember when I was five and Mom and Dad said they were practicing wrestling when I went into their room. They gave me peanut butter cookies and let me watch my favorite cartoon DVD. I ate so many cookies that I barfed."

Marsha's face reddened.

Lisa swatted Violet's shoulder. "It's not fair. I want Daddy to come back so I can play piggyback with him and eat peanut butter cookies and watch cartoons and learn how to wrestle."

Violet giggled. "Mom needs to teach you about the birds and bees."

"Why? Do they wrestle?"

"No, stupid. The acorns—" Her cheeks dimpled. "Never mind."

"I wish Daddy could sing the dolly song to me." Lisa pouted.

Marsha wiped her eyes. "I was cleaning out Daddy's dresser last night to give his clothes away, and I found something very special."

She led them to the sofa, opened the drawer in the coffee table, and pulled out a DVD with large black letters on the jewel case: *To All My Girls*. "This has a message from Daddy."

Marsha pushed the disc into the DVD player and plodded back to the sofa, where she sat with one daughter on each side.

She pressed the *Play* button on the remote control.

Paul's face appeared full-frame, freckle-brown hair in familiar disarray. He smiled the sexy smile that always turned Marsha's knees to mush, and started to talk, his baritone voice flooding the room with memories.

"I hope you never have to watch this video, but I know life can contain unexpected turns and detours. Now that I'm going to be a dad again, I want to create something special for all my girls. Just in case …"

Paul's chin quivered. "Hey, don't be sad. Violet and Marsha, I have many happy memories of you. And Lisa, I haven't met you yet, but you'll be born soon, and I know I'll have many happy memories of you too. Here's a song my mother used to sing to me and my sisters when I was little. Violet already knows it, and maybe you can learn it, too, Lisa."

He cleared his throat:

"My mamma told me
If I was goody
That she would buy me
A rubber dolly.

"Now don't you tell 'er
I found a feller,
Or she won't buy me
That rubber dolly."

Creases formed in Paul's brow. "I …" His voice broke. "I … wish … If you close your eyes real tight at night, then you'll hear me whisper in your ear when I tuck you in and give you a hug. Maybe you can play this sometimes, too, and remember how much your dad loves you. Marsh, I … wish I could tuck you in, too." He cocked his head and winked.

Marsha and the girls sobbed and smiled in unison, almost overpowering the sound of the recording, as Paul continued. "I love being a husband and a dad. I wouldn't give it up for anything, not for all the money or fame in the universe." He grinned and crossed his arms.

"Violet and Lisa, pay attention to your mom and do what she says. Eat your broccoli. It's healthy, and it makes you super smart. Keep your rooms clean. … Remember to say your prayers every night. Oh … Don't forget to brush your teeth. Mom will have enough worries without big dental bills, and when you join me someday, I want to see pretty smiles with no cavities."

His eyes seemed to twinkle as he moved so close that he blotted out the background. His lips formed a kiss, and he made a resounding smacking noise.

"I love you Marsha, Violet, and Lisa. I'll be thinking about you every minute from now until …" He sighed. "Well, we won't talk about that. I guess I said what I wanted to say. Now haul your butts away from the television and get some exercise. Keep healthy."

Paul waved, and the video faded to black.

Marsha thought she had shed all the tears she had left to give. But she was wrong. She hugged the girls, and the room filled with mournful wails from mother and daughters.

Finally, all that could be heard was the sound of soft snuffles.

Lisa squeezed Marsha's knee. "Now I can listen to Daddy sing the dolly song whenever I want."

Violet blew her nose. "Mom, could you cook broccoli for supper tomorrow?"

Lisa beamed. "Yes. Lots and lots of broccoli. With boy acorns in yours, Mommy. I want a baby brother."

Fat Chance

Granddaughter Violet struggles with a homework assignment.

Violet frowned. "Grandma, what does 'inflammable' mean?"

Megan poked the dimple in her granddaughter's chin. "If something is inflammable, it catches fire easily. Like the paper we use when you help Grandpa light a campfire. All it takes is a quick touch with a match, and it burns."

"That's what I thought. But it's also what 'flammable' means. If 'inactive' is the opposite of 'active', shouldn't 'inflammable' be the opposite of 'flammable'?"

"You'd think so, wouldn't you?" Megan studied Violet's serious face. She looked so much like her Grandpa Emmett with that wrinkled brow.

Violet pushed her notebook across the table and made a disgusted noise with her tongue between her teeth. "And when I make a campfire with Grandpa, we strike a match to make the fire, right?"

"Yes."

"And if I hit something, that's the same thing as striking it?"

"Yes."

"Then how come if I try to hit a baseball and miss it, the umpire calls it a 'strike'?"

Megan smiled. "Irony, I guess."

"But 'irony' doesn't have any iron in it, so where did the word come from?"

"Never thought of it that way, sweetie. Maybe you and I should invent our own language."

"Grandma, I'm serious." Violet scowled.

Megan laughed so hard she spilled coffee down the front of her dress. "Drat, that's hot. Much hotter and I'd have a first-degree burn."

"First-degree? I'll get the first-aid kit."

"No need."

"But that's like, boiling, right? On TV shows, first-degree murder is the worst kind."

"No. Burns are opposite. A first-degree burn is mild, and a third-degree one is serious. Look, just a little pink here on my upper chest. Nothing to worry about except getting the stain out before it sets."

"That's what you say about the sun when it goes down. It sets. Don't you want the stain to go away, like the sun at night?"

Megan tried to think of an answer.

"And what about 'caretaker'?" Shouldn't that mean someone who takes care away? But it means the same thing as 'care*giver*'. This English assignment is gonna kill me yet."

"That's why we have dictionaries. You can borrow mine if you want."

"I have one on my cell phone, but some words don't make any sense. Like 'ravel'. I looked it up already. It can mean to disentangle or to tangle. Two opposite definitions for the exact same word. How are people supposed to know what you mean when you write a story?"

"Pick a different word. That's the best solution."

"But I can't. Look."

Megan scrutinized her granddaughter's English assignment: *Write a composition using the following words: flammable, inflammable, caretaker, caregiver, and ravel.* She chuckled.

"Grandma, it's not funny!"

Megan's eyes twinkled. "When I was a kid, sometimes my dad would threaten to give me a good licking. But when I got into trouble with my mom, she'd threaten to give me a bad licking. When my butt got spanked, I didn't care what they called it. They both meant the same thing: I was in deep doo-doo."

"You got spanked? Wow, that must have been, like, centuries ago."

"Yup. When the dinosaurs roamed the earth and there weren't any video games."

Violet's eyes flashed, and she threw down her pen. "Will you help me?" She glanced at Megan's stern expression then bit her lip. "Please?"

"Slim chance of that happening. You need to figure it out on your own."

"Don't you mean 'fat chance', Grandma? You'll help me, right? So that makes the chance fat, not slim."

"Fat. Slim. Either way, it means the same thing. Check it out."

Violet pouted, but she picked up her pen and scrutinized the assignment. "I know what you mean, but that's another weird way of saying things. We 'check out' books from the library." She sighed. "Guess I won't get this done if I don't get going. And that's another one ... 'Get going'."

She looked up at Megan's pursed lips and lowered her eyes back to her paper. "I know. Just do it."

"Good girl. Break a leg."

"Grandma!"

Sleepie Soozie

It's Christmas, and everyone seems to be sold out of Sleepie Soozie dolls. What's a grandpa to do?

A short, skinny man in a green elf costume scampered through the mall toward Santa's throne, his arms piled high with colorful packages. He darted around a cell-phone kiosk, dodged a mother pushing a baby stroller, and collided with Emmett, who had moved in the same direction as the elf in an effort to evade him.

Presents flew every which way. Beads burst from one package. A wet stain appeared on another. A third, large and round, bounced into shoppers, who scattered like bowling pins. The rest landed in muddled disarray between feet, on top of a bench, and floating in the fountain.

The elf bit his lip. "I'm sorry, sir. Didn't mean to step on your toes. Are you all right?"

Emmett brushed liquid from his shirt and sniffed his fingers. *Smells like bubble goop.* "I haven't been all right for years. Sore back. Farsighted. Overweight. But my toes are fine."

The elf squinted and adjusted his hearing aid. "Pardon?"

Emmett yelled, "Just complaining about getting old, but looks like you got problems of your own. Here, let me help you."

"Thanks. I'll be late for my photos-with-Santa gig. Walt is gonna kill me."

"Walt?"

The elf whispered behind one hand, "Santa."

Emmett picked up the leaky package. "I'm Emmett, by the way."

The elf shook Emmett's hand. "Nice to meet you, Bennett. I'm Glenn."

Emmett thought about correcting Glenn, but changed his mind. Why bother? He'd probably never see the guy again.

They continued to scoop up presents. A friendly shopper tossed a basketball from inside a tree planter. Soon all the packages, including the broken ones, had been located. Glenn and Emmett transported them to Santa's throne.

Glenn grimaced. "Walt— er, Santa, I need to … go to the North Pole to return these and make a few more presents." He gave Santa a knowing look over the top of his glasses.

One of the kids standing in line raised his hand. "Mr. Elf, sir?"

Glenn bent toward him. "What can I do for you, little boy?"

"Can I go to the North Pole with you?"

Glenn smiled. "What's your name?"

"Billy, sir."

"Willy, do you know the magic words to summon Santa's sleigh?"

Billy shook his head.

Emmett propped his hands on his hips. "Well I do. I know all about magic stuff. And I'm going to be one of Santa's helpers today."

Billy's chin quivered, but he nodded and turned toward the throne. His face brightened as soon as Santa ho-ho-hoed and took the first child onto his lap.

Glenn motioned Emmett to the nearest exit. As soon as the kids were out of earshot, he dumped the broken gifts into a trash bin and groaned. "That accident is going to cost me. The mall association paid me a flat price for the gifts we're giving to the kids, and I have to replace them out of my own pocket."

"I thought you were just helping Santa."

"No. I'm a sales distributor. Every December I give special deals to malls. The elf gig is just a favor to Walt. We go way back."

Emmett pulled his wallet out and grabbed a couple of bills. "Here. I don't carry much cash, but this should help. If I hadn't been standing in the way gawking around for a Sleepie Soozie Hiccup Doll, you probably wouldn't have crashed into me."

"Hey, thanks! You got some real Christmas spirit."

By now, they had reached a large white van parked in the loading zone at the freight entrance. Glenn unlocked the back. "Let's see, four for girls and six for boys." He grabbed several gift-wrapped packages. "This should do it."

Emmett's gaze roamed over the piles of presents. "You sell stuff to other places too?"

"Yup. Gift shops and specialty retailers."

"That how you got your hearing aid?"

Glenn squinted and tapped one ear. "What?"

"Did you get your hearing aid from one of your suppliers?"

"Yeah. Might have to return it. I think it might be more than a battery problem."

Emmett nodded. "You sell to toy stores?"

"Toy stores, and ad—"

"Wouldn't happen to have a Sleepie Soozie Hiccup Doll, would you? We've been looking for one all over town. But everyone's sold out. It would make my wife so happy if I could find one."

Glenn adjusted his hearing aid again. "Damn thing." He smirked. "Gotta keep the wife happy, right? Let's see what I can find. Soozie, Soozie, where are you?"

He pushed several objects aside and rummaged until he found what he was looking for. "Here you go. I'll give you a good deal. We'll call it even for the cash you already gave me." He handed Emmett a package in a plain brown wrapper.

Emmett's eyes widened. "You sure? These things are going for a small fortune right now."

"Merry Christmas. Hope you enjoy it." He winked and gave Emmett a lopsided grin.

58

The men shook hands. Glenn rushed back into the mall, and Emmett climbed into his car.

Wait till I show Megan.

His cell phone rang, and he checked the call display. *Couldn't she wait until I got home?* "Hello, dear."

"Where are you? I've been waiting for half an hour."

"On my way. I'm just about ready to leave the mall."

"That's nice. We went shopping together, remember? I'm over by Walmart with a cartful of Christmas gifts."

"Crap. On my way."

He hurried toward Santa, who was listening to a freckle-faced girl with red hair. Her voice rang out, louder than the background music, "… and I want a Sleepie Soozie Hiccup Doll. The one with the blue dress."

Santa jiggled his leg up and down. "My elves are working overtime to make more Sleepie Soozies." He winked at the girl's parents. "But I don't know if we'll get them finished in time. Little girls all around the world are asking for these dollies."

She pouted, but accepted the candy cane he offered.

Santa pulled at his collar and wrinkled his forehead.

Emmett dawdled for a moment, touched by a tinge of guilt.

But not enough guilt to give away what he and Megan had been searching for so frantically.

~*~

Megan glared at Emmett as she climbed into the passenger seat and slammed the door with such force that the entire car shook.

Her stony silence finally ended with a voice that grated like barbed wire over a blackboard.

"I texted you several times, then I searched the whole mall and couldn't find you anywhere."

"Couldn't hear your texts over the mall music. Sorry."

"What were you doing?"

He motioned toward the back seat. "Just saving the day, like I always do. Found a Sleepie Soozie Hiccup Doll for Lisa."

His eyes searched hers for even a spark of Christmas spirit. "You can thank me later, if you know what I mean. Unless I fall asleep watching TV first."

Megan grimaced as she pulled the wrapping off the package. Then she broke into something bordering on hyena laughter, and wiped tears from her eyes.

He stared at her. "What you laughing at?"

"Guess you can skip television and go to bed early. Didn't you check this out before you bought it?"

"No ... Why?"

"It's a Sleezie Soozie Blowup Doll."

Dear Mister or Missus or Ms. NSA Director

Emmett decides to write a letter to the National Security Agency.

Hello? Hello? Testing … Testing … This hear is Emmett Walpole, composing a letter to the NSA while I try out my new dictation software. Heh heh. Might even get the letter done before I fix the dishwasher. Crap. Guess I shouldn't be thinking out loud. Blasted software is recording every word.

Select previous paragraph. Delete.

To The National Security Agency

I'll have to find the postal address later. Er … don't want that in the letter either.

Select previous paragraph. Delete.

Attention: Director

Dear Mister or Missus or Ms. NSA Director:

Re: My Personal Activities

I'm a retired blue-collar guy taking a creative writing course because I'm board, and I want to earn a few extra bucks. I also need an excuse to buy a big box of printer paper so I can hide my cigars in it.

What am I thinking? You already know all that. You probably know the size of my jockstrap, too. Extra-large, just in case you don't.

Anyway, I need to get in touch with you to discuss my recent activities. I noticed two of your men in dark suits and sunglasses tailing me last week. I tried to give them the slip by sneaking into a lingerie shop and going out the back door. But when I came out in the alley, they were waiting for me. At least I think they were the same guys. Hard to tell.

In case your wondering, the lace slip I had on my head was not an attempt to disguise my identity. It came off a wrack in the store when I dodged the next-door neighbor. Didn't want him to think I've got a thing for ladies' underware. Come to think of it, why in blazes was *he* in there?

Grate spell checker in this program. Oh, guess I shouldn't be running off at the mouth.

Select previous paragraph. Delete.

I decided to take the bull by the horns and contact you before you show up on my doorstep to arrest me. My wife, Megan, says it's my fertile imagination at work, or maybe my new allergy meds. Of course, you know Megan's name. You already know everything about me. So … Megan claims these guys are in town to promote a new movie. Just in case she's wrong though, I want to defend myself in advance of any legal—or illegal—actions you might plan to take against me. Not that you'd do anything illegal, right?

Know offense.

As I said, I'm trying to learn how to right good, and I often have to search the Internet for things in my stories. Those things might trigger your security flags. For instance, I'm writing a story about a person who blows up a building. When I searched for *bomb-building instructions* online, I certainly didn't intend to make one. A bomb, that is. All the fertilizer and chemicals in the shed are four the garden.

I'd never try to blow up my wife's stupid vegetable garden, despite all the bleepin' healthy crap she tries to makes me eat. Or the UPS store because they keep delivering the neighbor's packages to my house. Confidentially, I like to think of UPS as Useless Parcel Service. The neighbors might have heard me ranting in the back yard about UPS or broccoli, but honest, I'd never do any of the things I said.

The duct tape I bought isn't for a kidnapping or robbery, either. I need it to do a bunch of chores around the house. Stupid chores my wife keeps nagging me about. You should try duct tape sometime. Handyman's friend. Grate for fixing slippers, toilet seats, car bumpers. And even though I might think about muzzling my wife with it, I'd never carry threw. In fact, she always tells me I never carry threw with anything.

Oh, by the weigh, duct tape is good for making cat toys, too. Rip some tape off and scrunch it into little balls with the sticky side out and then watch your cat go crazy.

What did I want to say next? Lost my train. I do that sometimes. Park it and can't remember where I left it.

Select previous paragraph. Delete.

Let's talk about the social media business. I have no control over the people who send me friend requests on Facebook or those who follow me on Twitter. I accept the majority of friend requests. Where else can you tell people you farted after you ate breakfast? Or post pictures of your cat stuck to duct tape? Or give thumbs-ups to total strangers and tell them you like them?

I don't believe Donald Trump is an alien. Or that scientists have cloned Elvis. Or that John F. Kennedy and Marilyn Monroe are alive and well on a remote Pacific island. Although sometimes I wonder about Trump. His hair doesn't look human. Wonder if he's hiding an antenna under there. Maybe his hair *is* the antenna.

I follow Tweeters back most of the time, even though I think Twitter is a confusing and useless way to fritter my time. But I got lots of it. Time, that is. Besides, the more hours I spend online pretending to write, the better excuse I have not to fix the blasted dishwasher. Just between me and you, I do stuff to get my wife's goat. Or don't do it. Whatever.

To cut a long story short, I don't really mean the BS I share and say online. And please don't assume that I agree with the ideas or plans of my social media friends, whatever those ideas or plans might be. I'm pretty sure those people are all normal just like me. Hmm. Maybe not. Crap, they could all be cereal killers. Or aliens. How would I know?

Maybe I should get rid of my Facebook and Twitter.

Another thing I need to comment on is the Google auto-fill feature that keeps messing me up. When I begin typing something innocent such as *how to kill dandelions,* and Google inserts different words in the search bar, I can assure you I have know intention of producing weapons or poison powders, or murdering my wife.

No matter how much she nags.

Speaking of powder, if you find some on my letter, it's just silicone powder from my tackle box, not ricin or whatever the terrorists are using nowadays. Got it this afternoon via UPS. The silicone powder, that is. UPS finally did something right. I use the powder when I fish for trout to remove fish slime or water from a dry fly and reshape the hackle. Sprinkled some in my waders to soak up the moisture. Guess that's more information than I needed to share. You already know it, right?

All kidding aside, I got to close because I want to post this in today's mail, along with my subscription to *Flying Saucer Review*. That's a hole 'nother story.

I trust this letter finds you in good health.

Yours truly,

Emmett Walpole

Copies to: CSIS, MI5, ASIS, ISA

Megan's Maxims

*Here's another experimental piece of flash fiction known as a
listicle.*
Megan muses while Emmett is away fishing with the guys.

Patience is a virtue.

And when you're married to Emmett, you have to be patient. I
might even be the most patient woman on Earth—as my wet butt
can testify. Why can't he remember to put the toilet seat down? Or
to throw his toenail clippings in the trash? Or to carry his dishes to
the sink after he's finished eating? Last week when I was mucking
out the den, I found a half-eaten sandwich crawling with ants. He
says he loves me, but actions speak louder than words.

An apple a day keeps the doctor away.

Unless it's a rotten apple, swarming with fruit flies, in the garbage
I asked Emmett to take out. The freakin' things are everywhere,
including the butter dish. So much for waste not, want not. Had to
throw the butter away and use margarine to make sandwiches for
his fishing trip yesterday morning. He was in such a rush to get out
on the boat with his buddies he almost forgot to kiss me good-bye.
New rod, new tackle box, new hip waders …

A fool and his money are soon parted.

Ha! Except when it's time to repair the dishwasher. Emmett spun
his wheels for so long I figured the dishwasher would end up being
older than Methuselah before it started working again.
"Tomorrow," he said, "or the next day." Crap. Good thing I didn't
wait for him to tear himself away from the TV and fix it. I get so
mad at him sometimes. But that little twinkle in his eyes always
does me in just when I want to kill him. I love him. Nothing's
going to change that.

There's no fool like an old fool.

Especially when he's a stubborn old fool. He told me he could fix the dishwasher with a few parts from the hardware store. When? After I'm dead and buried? It broke down six months ago. Good thing I wasn't holding my breath while I waited for him to get his keister in gear. All it took *me* was half an hour on the Internet to figure out what to do. Ten minutes at the hardware store. Fifteen minutes of tinkering. Voila! If you need something done right, do it yourself. Translation: Get a woman to do it.

A woman's work is never done.

Dirty socks in the hallway. Toothpaste splattered all over the bathroom mirror. Muddy boot prints across the kitchen floor. Someone needs to remind Emmett that cleanliness is next to godliness. But it's easier said than done. God knows I've tried. Repeatedly. If he paid me a quarter for all the hours I spent cleaning up after him, I'd be a billionaire.

Old habits die hard.

Particularly when you're as stubborn as Emmett. Refuses to get rid of his LP records. Insists on keeping that tattered high school jacket he'll never fit into again. Won't throw away the pants he wore at grad even though they're umpteen sizes too small. Speaking of pants, what's this? Ha! Finders keepers, losers weepers. A fifty he forgot to take out of his pocket before he threw his jeans into the laundry. Ignorance is bliss, and what he doesn't know won't hurt me.

Look on the bright side.

I've had a quiet day with no bickering or nagging. I didn't have to pick up after Emmett or clean the bathroom mirror. Guess that's the bright part. But it's too quiet. I downloaded a novel to read this afternoon and then couldn't focus on the story. I even missed his cookie crumbs in bed last night. Guess I've been hard on him lately. Every man has his faults, and I'm not perfect, either.

Absence makes the heart grow fonder.

Wonder when he's getting back. He said by supper time, but that was two hours ago. The alarm app he bought for his cell phone was supposed to remind him when it was time to leave. Should I call him? Maybe not yet. It might embarrass him in front of the guys. I'll wait for another half hour.

Patience is a virtue.

Pills, Pills, Pills

Did you enjoy the previous listicle? Here's another one.
Emmett spends an afternoon browsing the Internet checking out
medications that might solve a few of his problems.

Blue Pill

Will help me "keep her up all night". Right. Until the heart attack that turns me into a corpse. Besides, Meg needs all the beauty sleep she can get. And what about the discomfort of keeping little Emmett up all night? But at least I'd die with a smile on my face. Heh heh. What about a pill that satisfies me so I don't have to bother with her? Although the cuddles are kind of nice. Especially in the winter. Awful getting old. Knees hurt. Little Emmett's shrinking. Can't read unless I hold a book two feet away.

White Pill

Would take care of the pain in my knees and back. What? I could only drink three beers a day? What about my fishing trips? We polish off half a dozen bottles before we leave the dock. And I have to "consult a doctor if the pain gets worse"? I thought this stuff was supposed to get rid of pain. No thanks.

Pink Pill

Won't have to wake up multiple times to pee. Humph. "May cause dry mouth, nausea, dry eyes, blurred vision" … and a whole bunch of other crap. Nothing about the heart, though. Blurred vision. Hey, that might come in handy when Megan sits across from me at the table, with her hair all over the place and that scowl on her face.

Pink-and-Blue Pill

Gets rid of toenail fungus. But I could lose my liver or kidneys, I'd have to give up booze, and it might cause a heart attack. Think I'd rather keep the old flaky nails. Nah, maybe not. Megan hates when I scratch her legs with 'em. Maybe I could soak them in kerosene. I'm pretty sure I read about that on one of the websites I visited yesterday. And kerosene would keep Sabrina from playing with my toes. Darned cat. Nail fungus and ticklish feet problems both solved. Without pills.

Purple Pill

This stuff is supposed to get rid of heartburn, but it "may cause nausea, vomiting, headaches, and heart arrhythmia". Heart arrhythmia. Humph. Do these drug companies spend all day trying to concoct stuff that'll damage my ticker? Good racket. They invent a pill that supposedly cures something, but it creates a whole bunch of other stuff. Then they sell you more pills to get rid of the new symptoms. I'd rather give up chili and tacos.

Red Pill

Multivitamins should be safe. Let's see. "Severe allergic reactions are possible, including rash, hives, itching, difficulty breathing, and chest tightness." What? Even multivitamins can cause heart problems? I'll eat more veggies and fruit. Megan's always nagging me about my horrible eating habits anyway. But the pizza and beer are so good. … Hey! Pizza's a vegetable. It has tomato sauce on it. And screwdrivers count as fruit. Problem solved.

Green Pill

Gets rid of gas. Should be pretty safe. Then I could drink all the milk and eat all the beans I want. Mind you, Megan doesn't like the belching and farting. If I don't take this, then I wouldn't have to use the blue pills to give little Emmett a boost, because Meg would refuse to come anywhere near me.

Another Pink-and-Blue Pill

This appetite suppressant looks interesting. It would help me stay away from all that fattening food that clogs up the old arteries. Blast. It contains caffeine. The doctor told me I have to avoid it. No point in giving up coffee and then taking something else that might be just as bad.

Yellow Pill

I reckon a sleeping pill is the answer. It'll help me sleep through the cravings and Megan's nagging. If my bladder gets too full, I'll wet the bed and not even know it. No need for purple pills to get rid of heartburn from all the food I won't eat. I can forget about the blue pills as well, because I'll be too sleepy to perform. Megan only needs one tablet to keep her up all night. Her freakin' computer tablet.

Anniversary Surprise

Emmett plans a surprise for their anniversary.

Emmett nodded, phone cupped to his ear. Two candles on the sideboard projected his flickering shadow onto the refrigerator. He repositioned a box of chocolates and bouquet of roses between the candles as he talked. Everything had to be perfect.

"Sure, Ger. I'm ready. 'You Light Up My Life' was the first song we danced to at our wedding. Just gotta feed the cat first. The back door's unlocked."

He hung up the phone and shook Sabrina's food dish. "Here, kitty, kitty, kitty. Suppertime." A blurry streak of Siamese cat dashed into the kitchen and brushed up against his leg.

Her purr was so loud he could hear it from his standing position. He reached down to scratch her chin. "Hey, what's that you got there? You been sleeping in Megan's underwear drawer again?"

Emmett pulled the black brassiere off Sabrina's head and set it on the table. "You hungry? Of course you are. Here we go."

She crouched over her food dish, tail twitching.

Emmett called toward the bedroom, "Sabrina stole one of your over-the-shoulder boulder holders again."

Megan sashayed toward him, eyes glinting in the candlelight, wearing nothing but a skimpy pair of black lace panties. "Too bad. It was supposed to be one of your presents for tonight."

His eyes bulged. And so did his boxers. "Uhhhh. I think …"

"Ooooooooh. I see you remembered our anniversary. I bought the bra and matching panties just for you. Too bad Sabrina spoiled my surprise."

Emmett pulled Megan close and whispered in her ear, "Yes, I remembered. I ordered food while you were in the shower. Take-out Chinese in the oven—all your favorites. Even left the back door unlocked so Gerry could sneak in with his violin."

"Oh, Emmett. There's a huge heart buried somewhere in all those insults you usually sling at me. I love you. What a nice surprise."

Sabrina bolted out of the kitchen and meowed at the back door.

Emmett's eyes widened. "I love you too. But that rustling behind you isn't Sabrina." The red embarrassment on his face deepened as he grasped at the tablecloth and tried to cover her. "Dinner wasn't the only surprise. Gerry just showed up with his violin."

Four Sides to Every Story

How did that puddle of yellow liquid get into the hallway?

A crash sounded from the direction of the kitchen. Megan glanced up from the sewing machine. "Emmett, did you break something? ... Violet, Lisa, was that you?"

The only sound she could hear was the drone of a nearby lawnmower. After listening for several seconds without receiving a reply, she called out again.

"Sabrina!"

The cat careened around the corner, struggling to maintain traction with claws that slipped over the newly waxed floor. Megan scratched behind Sabrina's ears and crooned, "Was that you, kitty-kitty?"

Sabrina stared up with unblinking eyes. "Meow."

"Were you playing with the spider plant again?"

"Meow." She rubbed against Megan's ankles.

Megan sighed. "Where's Emmett? He's supposed to be keeping an eye on the girls." She picked up the cat and strode toward the kitchen.

A sudden cold wetness soaked one of her socks. She yelled, "Who spilled in the hallway?"

Now, she didn't even hear the lawnmower. The house was quiet. Too quiet. *What is everyone up to?*

She dropped the cat, lifted her foot, and wiggled her toes. A small yellow puddle shone in the brightness of the hall light. "Sabrina, did you ...?" Megan supported herself against the wall while she removed the sock and sniffed. "Of course, you didn't. You never have accidents. What was I thinking?"

She hobbled toward the bathroom, toes of one foot raised. Thump step, thump step, thump step.

~*~

Violet's eyes widened. Grandma sounded angry. She gulped the last of her pineapple soda before slipping the empty bottle into the recycle bin, and then stole toward the hall closet.

I thought I was being so careful. I don't know how I spilled it. Will Grandma be upset if I clean up my mess and apologize?

She stopped and listened. Water ran in the bathroom sink. A neighbor's weed whacker buzzed. Whew! No Grandma. She rummaged in the closet for paper towels and spray cleaner.

~*~

Lisa bit her lip. Her bubbles had looked so pretty when she swept the bubble wand through the air, creating magical waves of little globes just like planets in outer space.

I was so, so careful. Will Gramma be upset I spilled my bubbles? I'll clean up the mess. Gramma says laziness is worse than telling fibs. I'll be un-lazy and un-fibsy.

She tiptoed into the kitchen and searched for the dishrag.

~*~

Emmett sighed. Had he screwed up again?

He checked the shrimp nectar in his bait box. His hand came away wet. And stinky. He must have spilled some in the hallway when he opened his UPS package and took the lid off the bottle. Better to man up now than have Meg nag all afternoon. He grabbed a handful of tissues and listened through the door of the den.

Gerry was mowing his lawn again. The fragrance of freshly cut grass wafted through the den window and almost overpowered the stench of shrimp on Emmett's fingers. Megan was still running water in the bathroom.

If I hurry, I can clean it up before she finishes.

He edged the door open and peered into the hallway.

~*~

Megan opened the bathroom door. Violet stood at one end of the hallway, paper towels and spray cleaner in hand, frowning. Lisa stood at the other end, looking from the dish rag in her hand to the hallway floor, as though she had lost something. Emmett clutched a handful of tissues, his other hand on the den door, a quiver in his chin.

Megan gazed from face to face, and then laughed. "Is it Mother's Day? Or my birthday? It's so nice that all three of you volunteered to clean up my apple juice mess."

Valentine Verdict

Megan shops for a Valentine card.

Can't believe I've been with the old coot forty-two Februarys. What kind of Valentine should I choose? Funny or serious?

So many to pick from. Pop-up, holographic, musical— No way I'm getting a singing card. Emmett hates them.

Although this one with the "Wild Thing" soundtrack and a burly guy in leathers next to a motorbike looks interesting. Emmett keeps asking for a Harley, but I'm too scared to let him buy one since Paul's accident. … Maybe— Crap, that's loud! Nope. Music is definitely out. Besides, one look at this, and he might start making googly eyes at motorcycles again.

Here's one with a bouquet of roses and violets on front. Sort of like the flowers he gave me at grad. Ah, the good old days. Gas was cheap, we could still make out in the drive-in, and nobody was glued to cell phones or computer tablets. The grandkids don't know what they're missing.

What's happening to the world? By the time Violet and Lisa learn to drive, they'll have to mortgage their left arm and liver to buy a tank of gas. They hardly talk anymore. It's all e-mail and Facebook and Twitter.

Guess I should stop bellyaching about stuff I can't change and look inside.

Violets are blue,
Roses are red,
I love you a lot,
'Specially in bed.

Sounds like something a horny teenager would say. Or something I might have said way back when. Where do they find the airheads who write these rhymes? In high school?

Oh, I like this. A silhouetted couple embracing on the beach. Beautiful artwork with seagulls and starfish. Reminds me of our honeymoon. I can almost hear the swish of the waves and smell the kelp wrapped around our toes. And Emmett pulling me close, then hiding in a quiet cove while we … Makes me tingle just thinking about it.

> *I think about you*
> *every moment, every day.*
> *You inspire me, complete me,*
> *in every way.*
>
> *We've been through a lot,*
> *two as one,*
> *But our life together*
> *is still not done.*
>
> *I cherish each kiss,*
> *each soft embrace,*
> *And when I dream,*
> *I see your face.*
>
> *You're my love, my all,*
> *my shining knight.*
> *In your sturdy arms,*
> *the world is bright.*

This is too freakin' mushy. I'd never talk like that, and Emmett knows it.

Here's one with an hourglass on the cover. Strange graphic for a Valentine.

> *The sands of nature*
> *sift and flow*
> *Our bodies age,*
> *our brains grow slow*
> *The wrinkles deepen,*
> *aches increase ...*

Ugh. That's too damn depressing. Won't even finish reading it. Let's see …

A couple cuddled up in a porch swing. Looks like *our* swing. It's even green like ours. Blank inside. Yup, *this* is the one that I want.

The one that I want—ha ha. Makes me think of that song from *Grease*. We were married five years when it came out. Necked in the back row of the theater on our anniversary. Had to return and see the movie again the following week because we missed so much of it.

~*~

Twenty minutes of thinking and rethinking and writing, and this is the best I can do? Crap. Let me give it one more try.

~~Emmett,~~

It's Valentine's. I can do better than that.

Dearest Emmett,

~~You always tell me you don't have conversations with me because you don't want to interrupt my nagging~~

That's not a very good beginning. But he's right about the nagging. Okay, I think I've got it.

Dearest Emmett,

I know I nag too much. It's because I'm frustrated about getting old. But I'm growing old with you, and that makes me happy. You make me happy. If I had to do it all over again, I'd marry you in a heartbeat.

Happy Valentine's Day, sweetie.
All my love,
Megan

Road Trip

Emmett plans a getaway.

Emmett pointed to a sign just off the highway. "Look at that one: *Trespassers will be shot. Survivors will be shot again.* Funniest one we've seen so far."

Megan grimaced. "Quit it. You won't make me laugh." She shook her head. "You and your cheapskate getaway ideas."

He took his eyes off the traffic for a second to grin at her. "C'mon. It'll be fun. Just you an' me and the guys at the fishing cabin. You've gotta learn to relax."

She wrinkled her nose. "Why would I want to spend a week in a stinky cabin?"

"The fish don't stink. We keep them on ice."

"I'm not talking about the fish. I mean the sweaty armpits, cigars, and ripe socks. Not to mention the farts after you guys fill up on beans."

Emmett rolled his eyes. "It can't be any worse than that stinky gruyere cheese you fry up with potatoes."

"Swiss fried potatoes? You eat it when I cook it. And then you lick your fingers. And scrape out the frying pan. It can't be that bad."

"Yeah, well, it reeks. And when I'm starving, anything tastes good."

Megan poked his stomach. "You? Starve? With that paunch, you could go without food for forty days and forty nights."

"I'm not—" Emmett jammed on the brakes. "Idiot driver!" He rolled down his window and yelled at the car ahead of them, "The sign says 'Yield', not 'Give Up'. Move your butt, buddy."

He took his foot off the brake and eased forward, honking along with the angry chorus from the rest of the traffic. "Speaking of farts, did you know smelling them is good for you? Sniffing hydrogen sulfide could help prevent mito … kon … cell damage."

"You and your goofy ideas. What the heck are you talking about this time?"

"I read it on the Internet. Some bigwig university in the UK did a study on it. It might even help cure cancer."

"Then as long as I stay married to you, I should live forever. And ever. And ever."

He bit his lip. "I can't help it if milk gives me gas."

"You didn't have any milk last night or this morning, did you?"

"No … why?"

"You've been farting ever since we left the house."

"I'm sorry. I was trying to be quiet."

"Quiet? You need a hearing aid, honey. And maybe you should get your sniffer checked out too." She glared at him. "You were nibbling on the gruyere cheese again, weren't you?"

His ears turned red. "Maybe."

She squeezed his knee. "Admit it. You like that cheese, even if it stinks."

"Maybe."

"And I like you. Even when you stink."

He choked on a chuckle. "Is that another way of saying you love me?"

"Maybe."

Emmett pointed to the dash. "Guess I'd better fill up. We're down to a quarter tank."

"For crying out loud! Did you forget to fill up before we left town?"

"Maybe."

She glowered at him, lips pressed into a thin, angry line.

He pretended not to notice and pulled into Barney's Groceries & Gas. He continued to ignore her stony displeasure as he swiped his credit card and watched a greasy-looking guy in the next lane while he filled up. The kid's pants hung so low they looked like they might slide down to his ankles any second.

Emmett stared, with no attempt to hide his disgust.

The boy frowned.

Emmett continued to eye the kid as he crawled back into the driver's seat. He shook his head. "Kids today got no fashion sense. Either that, or he has an advanced degree in stupid."

"Emmett! He might hear you."

"Nah. He's plugged into his music. Couldn't hear a foghorn unless you hit him over the head with it."

She stuck out her tongue. "You could try to be polite once in a while."

"Nag, nag, nag. Why should I be polite? Everyone expects old people to be crotchety and outspoken. Let's see how far we can push him." He activated the power window button, but changed his mind when he spied the darts in Megan's eyes. "Or not. Let's grab an ice cream cone. It's so hot in here my sweat is sweating."

He tugged at his collar.

Megan's eyes narrowed. "Ice cream? Ice cream! What are you up to? You look as guilty as a raccoon rummaging in the strawberry patch."

He grinned. "Can't get anything by *you*, can I?" He steered the car into a parking lot next to a nearby convenience store. "C'mon, I have something to show you. Keep your eyes closed until I tell you to open them."

He walked around the car and helped her out, leading her by the elbow. "No peeking."

"Emmett?"

"Trust me."

"I've heard that line before … and nine months later, Marsha was born."

"Just a few more feet. Watch out for the rock. Okay. Stop. Turn to your left. There. Now you can open your eyes."

Megan blinked. A rusty old car with a sky-blue body and white top sat just a few feet away. "This looks like the car you had when we … There's a dent on the rear panel. In exactly the same place where I hit a garbage can when I was trying to parallel park on Willow Street."

"It doesn't *look* like the car. It *is* the car. My '56 Chevy Bel Air 4-door. The one we took on our honeymoon."

"Oh, sweetie. … Wherever did you find it?"

"The guy who bought it from me stored it in a barn. Never drove it. When he died, his family sold it in an estate sale. I recognized it from the dent and bought it back. What do you think?"

Her eyes misted. She clutched Emmett's hand. "Sure brings back memories. Is it drivable?"

"Yup. How do you think it got here? Motor's a bit rough, but it still runs. My fishing buddies helped me. They do lots more than just burp and fart, you know."

Megan opened the passenger door and rummaged around in the glove compartment. "I wonder …" She pulled out a Twinkie, still in its plastic wrapper, complete with little cowboy and lasso under a 15¢ price tag.

She opened the bag, split the ghastly ash-gray cake in two, and offered half to Emmett. They both examined the cream-filled treat and sniffed before taking a tentative bite.

Megan looked like she had just eaten the sourest pickle in the universe. "Yuck. I always wondered if the old stories about these things keeping forever were true."

Emmett smirked. "Better than the cake I tried to bake for your birthday."

She reached into the glove compartment again and pulled out a condom. "Guess what else I found. If you hadn't misplaced this, Marsha might never have happened."

Emmett smiled, but he couldn't hide the moistness in his eyes. "I'm glad I lost it." He pulled her close for a kiss and whispered in her ear, "Wanna try it again, for old time's sake?"

"In the middle of the day?" She squeezed his behind before pulling away with a suggestive curl of her tongue.

"You're sending mixed signals."

"Not here!"

"Alrighty then. Let's transfer our luggage into this old jalopy and hit the road."

"Really? *Really?* You still intend to take me to that stinky fishing cabin?"

"Nope. You didn't really think I was serious about that, did you? Gerry and Ray are gonna be here in a few minutes to drive the Malibu home. Booked a B&B for the week. Only five minutes away."

He scooped her up into his arms. "Let's go, woman, while my motor's running. I'm still young at heart, but slightly older elsewhere, and I didn't bring any little blue pills with me."

"I love you, sweetie."

"Love you too, hun."

Free Stories

The following stories are from Kathy's anthology *Suppose: Drabbles, Flash Fiction, and Short Stories*, which is available in digital and print format at numerous outlets.

Schud Justice

Sometimes justice lurks in the hands of a jilted woman. Just ask Fronn Husten.

"Halt. Now!"

"Stop, or we'll shoot."

The demands of two deep voices accompanied the drum of determined footsteps.

The target of the voices, a spindly, thin-lipped alien, tossed a stolen purse. "You have to catch me firssst."

He scrabbled into an alleyway before his pursuers could shoot or stun him.

They searched and probed every corner.

A beefy man with a humongous wart on his nose sighed. "Guess he got away." He returned his laser blaster to its holster. "Don't know how. It's a dead end. Stupid Schud should stay where he belongs: in a swamp."

His scrawny partner with the bug eyes snickered at the *shood shood* remark. Then he looked up. "You'd have to be an arachnibot to reach those windows."

Fronn Husten crouched in the garbage bin. Flies nibbled at the sweat on his forehead. He held a hand over his nose until the men left. Then he sneezed … and sneezed … and sneezed. He swore with a sibilant hiss. "Ssuffering croakers. Chocolate. There's chocolate ssomewhere in here. Sstupid Earthlings and their candies." He hoisted himself out of the bin and horked into a Freshnnex tissue.

Then he strode east, with focused resolve, sneezing every few steps. He had memorized the address of the woman who owned the purse. She had what he wanted, and he intended to get it.

Now.

~*~

Oceane Kozmire finished applying her makeup and stepped away from the mirror to admire the results. That should do it. She approved of the honey-beige lipstick. Mmm. Even tasted like honey. With a hint of chocolate. She wanted at least a couple more tubes. Whenever she found a color she liked on one of these primitive planets, the manufacturer discontinued it. "No time like the present," she whispered.

Although she had other reasons besides lipstick for leaving her condopodium.

~*~

Fronn Husten trailed Oceane, but any passersby who bothered to look would have seen a female instead of a male. A study in dull: androgynous outfit and hairstyle; thin, frog-like lips; sensible shoes. Hives covered his face, and bouts of sneezing still wracked the little alien's frame. He used up a complete pack of Freshnnex before he started to dry his nose on his sleeve.

Oceane picked up her pace. Her heels clicked faster and faster on the sidewalk.

Fronn waited for just the right moment. Then he forced her into an alley and waved a blaster in her face. "Not a ssound, or I'll use this. Achoo! Achoo!"

For a microsecond, she seemed to grin. No, maybe not. A vein throbbed in her neck as she raised her hands.

His gawk glued itself to her purse. "How many purses you got? This isn't the one you had before."

"What's it to you?"

He shoved her and rifled through the purse's contents. "Where is it?"

"Where's what?"

"The CashCard you used this afternoon at Yasmine's Boutique."

"At home, I suppose."

"Then we'll just go get it. Right now." He turned her toward the street, with the blaster in his pocket aimed at her back. "Get moving."

When onlookers saw Oceane walking home followed by a diminutive woman in beige a half step behind her, they paid no attention. They were too busy listening to their audio devices, watching holovids on their glasses, and playing games on their wrist consoles.

Ten minutes later, Fronn forced Oceane to open the front door of her condopod. He glanced around with wary eyes to make sure nobody in the street was paying any attention to them. *Like Earthlings would notice anything except their gadgets. They're a dumb lot.* He pushed her onto the sofa. Bound and gagged her.

Then he sorted through the items on the kitchen counter. Ah, there it was. His counterfeit Intergalactic CashCard. He removed it and replaced it with the one in his wallet. *Our cards must have got mixed up at Yasmine's. I've gotta give up my fondness for women's underwear. But the silk feels so good.* He emptied the dirty tissues from his pockets and grabbed a full pack of Freshnnex as he headed toward the exit.

His head felt woozy. He leaned against a wall for a moment and closed his eyes.

The wooziness disappeared. And so did his sneezing.

~*~

Fronn slipped into his secret love nest and switched on the computer.

He waited for his specialized software to load, glowering and drumming a solo with his fingertips. After several seconds, he inserted the fake CashCard into an adapter and left the computer running while he brewed fresh coffee. Earth computational systems were slow and inefficient. The process would take several hours.

In the meantime, he planned to put up his feet and watch the news on the holovid. He had a hopeless fan crush on the anchorperson: a human woman with sexy eyes and a mesmerizing voice. *I bet she wears silk underwear.*

Monday night. The best night to catch up on intergalactic updates. He cocked his head. *Hmm. No more sneezing or hives. Remarkable recovery.* Usually it took at least a day to get back to normal after he'd been exposed to chocolate. He shrugged and leaned toward the holovid.

"It is now Tuesday, 1800 hours. Time for the Intergalactic News Report …"

He swiped to pause the live feed. Frowned. Restarted at the beginning of the broadcast.

"It is now Tuesday, 1800 hours. Time for the Intergalactic News Report …"

He looked at his computer calendar and cursed. "Ssuffering croakers. I've lost a day. A whole day. Sson of a sspace ssow. Felizitas will never forgive me." He grimaced and squinted, trying to determine what had caused his memory lapse.

~*~

Oceane touched her earlobe communicator. "Initial phase of mission accomplished. Please advise Felizitas Husten that the assignment is proceeding as planned."

She glanced at one of the holovids in her living room. "It was easy to implant a camera in Fronn's visual cortex after he inhaled through the specially prepared Freshnnex. It took me several hours longer than expected to install and test. Schud eyes are always a challenge. But the observation feed is working flawlessly. We can see everything he sees. He'll be disoriented at first, although I'm sure he'll adjust. Agent 3.111-238 out."

She smiled at the beefy agent with the humongous wart on his nose and nodded to the scrawny operative with the bug eyes.

"Good idea chasing the Schud into a trash bin. Too bad you had to let him escape. Trash. That's where every Schud should be."

~*~

Fronn rewound the holovid several times. *Exactly twenty-four hours. I've lost twenty-four hours. But that's impossible. I must be confused. Yesterday was Monday and today is Tuesday.* He scowled. *Of course. I'm just a bit confused.*

He slouched into the soft curvature of the sofa. *So relaxing. So tired.* He scratched several times out of habit, even though he wasn't itchy. Then he drifted off to sleep.

Oceane's observation feed turned dark.

~*~

Felizitas Husten swatted at screen after screen of photos. Fronn with an Earth woman. Fronn with another Earth strumpet. Fronn with a Schudalian lush. Fronn with an Erpisonnian streetwalker. "Son of a frog. You won't get away with this, you miserable little snake of a cheater, you."

She continued to review Oceane's evidence.

Fronn, a typical Schudalian, wasn't the smartest alien in the cosmos. Schudalians, called Schuds by most in the Intergalactic Alliance, weren't the most attractive of aliens either. Their thin lips and skinny legs were reminiscent of Earth frogs: creatures that had died out centuries previously due to widespread droughts.

But a male Schudalian's skill in the bedroom, augmented by saliva with aphrodisiac properties, intoxicated his lovers. Enamored females paid no attention to the repulsiveness of the knobby, groping fingers and snake-like tongues.

These ugly aliens were detested for their elaborate swindles and scams; for their trickery and deception. To be called a Schud was considered the ultimate insult on many planets.

Schuds liked Earth. There was hardly any chocolate on the planet since the blight that had wiped out the Theobroma cacao trees in the twenty-third century. Fronn's species was horribly allergic to the stuff. The slightest exposure, even to a chocolate wrapper, caused itchy hives and sneezing. However, few humans bought chocolate anymore. Nowadays it was produced on the planet Erpisonn. The prohibitive shipping cost made it unaffordable for most people.

Felizitas reached the last photo.

The look she gave the walls would have shattered blaster-proof glass. "How could I have joined with a Schudalian? Me, an Earth woman, joining with a Schud? Was I stupid?"

Felizitas glared at her screen. "I was in love with you, Fronn. But not anymore. You'll be sorry. I'll see that you wind up where every Schud should be: in prison."

~*~

Midnight. Fronn woke with a start. *I wonder if the computer's finished.* Yes, there it was. Line after line after line. The largest phishing database in the universe. Credit card numbers, financial information, dark secrets that could be used for blackmail. A Schud's dream. He swiped at his screen.

Whose number should I use first? Doesn't matter.

> "Sspiffy, sspoofy, find a schmo.
> Phish a man with lotsssa dough.
> If limit's high, make him pay
> Heaps of credits every day."

He intended to indulge in every one of his expensive tastes and fetishes, and maybe some new ones.

~*~

Fronn Husten didn't return to Felizitas. He bought fine silk underwear from the most expensive suppliers. He rented the services of a high-class escort, who accompanied him wherever he went in his new aerolimo. He frequented exclusive roof-top restaurants and private spas, and purchased jewelry made of rare gems set in platinum. In fact, he lived like an emperor for one day short of one terrestrial month.

Then Earth police beat down his door and arrested him.

~*~

Oceane touched her earlobe communicator. "Ready to beam up in five minutes."

She dismantled her holovid equipment as she spoke to her fellow agents. "Pity to leave Earth. I've enjoyed it here. Poor Fronn. Guess he didn't appreciate The Agency filling his phony card with the financial information of every intelligence official and CEO on the planet. I'm sure the final straw, so the Earthlings say, was his fraudulent access to the Intergalactic CashCard CEO's account."

She chortled.

~*~

And what became of Fronn?

The judge who presided over his trial had a warped sense of humor. She sentenced him to ten years of hard labor in a factory. On Erpisonn. Good climate. No computers. Billions of Theobroma cacao trees and thousands of chocolate factories.

Felizitas Husten hired The Agency for one more assignment: to locate all of Fronn's secret bank accounts.

When she filed for official unjoining, she liquidated the considerable assets she received as settlement. Then she bought the chocolate factory where Fronn worked, and took over as manager.

Revenge was sweeter than the finest chocolate.

Somnus Interruptus

This is a drabble: a story of exactly one hundred words.
"A use has been found for everything but snoring." ~ Mark Twain

"You were snoring again," Josie mumbled. "Roll over. I need my sleep. Bobby has Tiny-Tots soccer at seven."

"I was not snoring." Vern pulled the covers up to his chin.

"Yes, you were." *I don't know if I can survive another night like this. Why won't he see the doctor?*

Josie's restless dreams teemed with grinding gears, rumbling freight trains, and snarling tigers.

Early in the morning, long before dawn had touched the sky, Bobby climbed into their bed. "Mommy, I'm scared. Could I please sleep with you? My room is too quiet, and Daddy's growling keeps the monsters away."

Traffic Violation

Have you ever been stopped by a police officer for a moving-traffic violation?

Flashing lights. The yelp of a siren. Motorists craning their necks.

Quentin Parsons frowned and squinted at the police car in the rearview mirror as he slowed to a stop. He rolled down the window and waited with white-knuckled fists on the steering wheel. "What's the problem, officer?"

The cop looked young, probably fresh out of training, and although her square jaw emoted determination, the softness of her Bambi eyes and a nervous tug at an earlobe spoiled the resolute impression. She spoke with a tremor in her voice. "Driver's license and registration, please."

"But officer, I—"

"Now!" She kept her hand on her holster while he rifled through the papers in the glove compartment.

He loosened his tie and sized her up as he perused her name tag. "Here, Officer Kenise. I think you'll find everything in order."

She paused to listen to her personal radio. Her face paled, and she stuffed his documentation into a pocket. "Out of the car and down on the ground."

"But—"

"NOW!"

No matter how righteous a person's case, you don't argue with a loaded gun. Quentin's face greeted the pavement with a haste he hadn't mustered since his last college-football touchdown. Even as he tried not to wreck his well-worn navy suit, he suspected that both knees would now betray their encounter with the asphalt.

Officer Kenise called for backup.

Squad cars appeared from both directions and squealed to a stop. Police personnel piled out. Three hulks thudded closer, hands on their weapons, and conferred with Kenise.

The sound of honking horns filled the afternoon air, and the stench of burnt rubber wafted over from one of the police cars. Quentin hoped they wouldn't pop his trunk.

They did.

Blood-stained sheets. Shovel. Vials containing a viscous, red liquid.

"You're under arrest." Kenise handcuffed him and read him his rights.

"But I can explain."

"Explain it to the judge."

"I was on my way to—"

"No matter where you *were* going, *now* you're on your way to lockup."

~*~

Quentin spent two hours sharing a holding cell with a pair of cockroaches. Seconds seemed like days as the pressure in his bladder increased. But he couldn't force himself to use the dirty-looking toilet in plain view of anyone who happened to walk by.

Finally, Officer Kenise returned. She forced her face into an awkward smile. "Mr. Parsons, your paperwork checks out. I've been ordered to apologize. Something about keeping you happy so you don't sue us for false arrest."

She scratched her chin. "But I'd like to explain why I arrested you. You matched the description of someone who's wanted for murder, and the evidence in your trunk certainly seemed incriminating at first. Why were you carrying vials of cranberry juice, and sheets stained with pigs' blood?"

Quentin shrugged. "As I attempted to tell you, I was on my way to a wedding. The bride and groom are into this zombie-apocalypse thing, and they have a reception arranged for after the service. The stuff in my trunk was for props."

Kenise laughed. "That explains it. And I suppose it's going to be a *dead* reception full of *stiffs*, with people *dying* to get in."

He grinned. "Funny lady."

Her smile disappeared. "Sarge practically chewed me a new …" Her face reddened.

"Don't worry about me suing the police department. But if I were you, I *would* worry about what the Chief might do when your sergeant fills him in on the details."

"He'll be in a good mood, because his son got married this afternoon."

Quentin smirked. "I don't think so. I'm the minister."

Tech Support

Here's another drabble.

When was the last time you called tech support? Did you wait

forever on hold?

"Press one for support—" BEEP

"Stupid menus. Where the heck are the people?" ...

"Good afternoon. This is Larry. How may I help you?"

"I didn't call the dairy."

"LARRY, ma'am."

"Larry, you've sent the wrong color. Again. I asked for white, but that's not what you shipped."

"We'll fix that. Any other problems?"

"Aside from the flimsy construction?"

"Customer code, please?"

"A-532283."

"I'm sorry, but I can't find you in the system."

"Your telephone support is as rotten as your stocking support."

"Stockings? Ma'am, I think you've called the wrong number. This is Foundation Electronix, not Foundation Sox."

MUDD

Beauty products come in a wide range of prices, but quality is always more expensive. Would you be willing to pay for the best mud treatment in the county?

August is the best month: the month after local creeks and rivers overflow, depositing generous accumulations of sediment. Mallory, co-proprietor of Mallory and Ursula's Dirty Delights Spa, a.k.a. MUDD, loves the feel of mud on her fingers. Her hands are always smooth and soft, her fingernails long and strong. She and her harvesters haul the mud from Sludge Flats to the spa. There they add volcanic ash, seaweed, clay, mineral water, and an essential-oil mixture that neutralizes the unusual smell.

Clients luxuriate in 102° MUDD-baths, cucumber slices over their eyelids, ecstatic to discover the improvement in their skin and muscle tone. Over the years, the price for a MUDD-bath has doubled, tripled, quadrupled. And nobody complains. The price is worth it, everyone says.

Mallory and Ursula's bank accounts continue to bulge, and they wallow in the good life.

~*~

Every summer, retired plumber Jed Rentner watches birds and hikers from the creaky rocking chair on the porch of his retirement cabin in the woods. The wizened geezer is always happy to talk to strangers. Nobody can tell whether his stories are true, but his visitors sit around him on wooden chairs, sometimes for hours. His favorite tale is about his flush outhouse. The only one in the county, he claims.

"Yep. I kid you not. Happens every year. My outhouse is just yonder, over there beside the road into town. In June when the runoff's high, muddy water floods everythin' out here. It raises the water table and fills my outhouse to ground level. By August, the crapper's clean and empty. Just a little silt and mud in the hole. Even smells good."

He cracks a toothy grin and pokes at his teeth with a toothpick. "Yep. Sweet smellin' and maintenance-free."

Today's rapt listener is Sonja, a frequent customer of Mallory and Ursula's Dirty Delights Spa. She scowls. "But your cabin is right above Sludge Flats, isn't it?"

"Now that you mention it, s'ppose it is."

"You don't mean—" She recoils.

"Sure do. I s'ppose one of these days I should tell those girls where their mud comes from. Maybe old Jed should be gettin' a royalty."

Afterword

You haven't seen the last of Megan and Emmett's family. They're on vacation right now, relaxing and getting into more trouble. I'll tell you all about it in the next Megan and Emmett anthology.

I'd like to talk to you now about reviews.

Positive comments and ratings help authors earn a living. After you reach the end of this book, I urge you to post a review. If you didn't like what you read, please get in touch and tell me why. I'll try to address your concerns:

Author@KathySteinemann.com

And remember Joseph Addison's observation: "Reading is to the mind what exercise is to the body."

Keep reading.

About the Author

Kathy Steinemann, Grandma Birdie to her grandkids, is an award-winning author who lives in the foothills on the Alberta side of the Canadian Rocky Mountains. She has loved words for as long as she can remember.

As a young child, she scribbled poems and stories. During the progression of her love affair with language, she won public-speaking and writing awards, and she contributed to her school newspaper. Then every Monday, rain or shine, she walked home instead of taking the bus so that she could deliver her latest column to the community weekly.

Her career has taken varying directions, including positions as editor of a small-town paper, computer-network administrator, and webmaster. She has also worked on projects in commercial art and cartooning.

Her books include *IBS-IBD Fiber Charts*, *Top Tips for Packing Your Suitcase*, the *Sapphire Brigade* series, and several others.

Kathy's Website
KathySteinemann.com

Books by Kathy Steinemann

- Nag Nag Nag: Megan and Emmett Volume I

- Suppose: Drabbles, Flash Fiction, and Short Stories

- The Doctor's Deceit: Sapphire Brigade Book 2

- Vanguard of Hope: Sapphire Brigade Book 1

- The IBS Compass

- Top Tips for Packing Your Suitcase

- IBS-IBD Fiber Charts

- Practical and Effective Tips for Learning Foreign Languages

- Life, Death and Consequences

- Leben, Tod und Konsequenzen (German Edition)

- Matthew and the Pesky Ants

- Matthias und die verflixten Ameisen (German Edition)

- Top Trips for Travel by Air

~*~

You have reached the end of the book. Thank-you for reading. If you enjoyed it, please recommend it to a friend and review it online.

www.ingramcontent.com/pod-product-compliance
Lightning Source LLC
Chambersburg PA
CBHW071614040426
42452CB00008B/1337